Le

"Finally, a parenting manual that ~~...y... ...~~ not exist. This simple, to the point, and useful resource is a must for every parent."

—Al Estee, founder, Social Emotional Learning Alliance for South Carolina

"Through a series of illustrative vignettes, Donavan demonstrates a manageable way of controlling the emotions that too often complicate interpersonal communication. Ultimately, *Let, Lift & Listen* is about attitude, namely, how to treat your children with respect and dignity, even as you and they endure the trials of childhood and adolescence."

—Dr. Kevin T. Kalikow, MD, child and adolescent psychiatrist, author of *Your Child in the Balance* & *Kids on Meds*

"Christine Donavan knocks it out of the park with this elegant and concise book. It is full of not only great principals of parenting but real-world applications of these principles that we can all relate to. Her knowledge and years of first-hand experience shines through to help us and walk with us on our parenting journey. I will be recommending it to my clients and using it at home."

—James McKinney, MD, child and adolescent psychiatrist

"*Let, Lift, & Listen* is a great resource for parents, no matter the age of your children. It's filled with time-honored wisdom as well as practical stories of how to apply the 3-step framework in a wide variety of situations."

—Thomas Hughes, co-lead pastor of Christian Assembly Church Los Angeles, author of *Down to Earth: How Jesus' Stories Can Change Your Everyday Life* and *Curious: The Unexpected Power of a Question-Led Life*

"*Let, Lift and Listen* captures the fundamentals for parenting....these profound and basic skills apply throughout our lives.

—Robert Chapman, founder of Chapman Foundation for Caring Communities, CEO of Barry Wehmiller; author of *Everybody Matters*

"Parenting is a hard job...but it might be easier than we think if we use a few basic principles outlined in this book. Chris's wisdom and experience guide us through real-life examples to illustrate how some simple shifts in our own behaviors can influence children's actions."

—**Angela W. Williams, MAT, Educator, The Citadel,**
CEO, Custom Communication & Coaching,
Communication Consultant, Author of *Hush Now, Baby*

A Timeless Framework for Effective,
Guilt-Free Parenting of all Ages and Stages

Let, Lift, & Listen

CHRISTINE DONAVAN
CERTIFIED PARENT COACH

Editing, design, and distribution by Bublish
Published by Kids on the Go Corporation

ISBN: 978-1-887077-01-9 (eBook)
ISBN: 978-1-887077-00-2 (paperback)

To Mom and Dad, who believed in me,
encouraged me, and loved me well.

Making the decision to have a child is momentous.
It is to decide forever to have your heart go
walking around outside your body.

—Elizabeth Stone

CONTENTS

PREFACE

Suzanne and Cliff sat awkwardly in my office. The discomfort of asking for help was overshadowed only by the tension between them, fueled by disagreements on how to discipline their sixteen-year old daughter, Sophia, and their twelve-year-old son, Nate. The yelling, the punishments, the lectures—nothing was working, and things were getting worse. In her initial phone call, Suzanne struggled to hold back tears as she described the chaos in their home: the constant yelling, the bickering, and, often, the silent treatment among all members of their family. Suzanne had even expressed concerns about the state of her marriage. The stress had taken its toll. Her perception was that her husband was either too harsh or completely absent. Later, Cliff confided in me his belief that Suzanne was too soft on their children, often failing to follow through on her threats and frequently coming to Nate and Sophia's defense.

Isaac and Elisha were feeling lost and uncertain. After years of desperately wanting a child, they now had three-year-old Jacob, who was more than they could handle. It seemed that the preschooler had taken over their lives as they realized that making a baby was only the beginning of a lifetime journey of learning for the new parents. Their second baby was due in just four months, and they felt inadequate and unready. They longed to be the best parents they could be but felt like they were failing. Little Jacob seemed to dictate their every move, and they could not imagine dealing with another newborn.

Zach and Ashley were beginning a second marriage with his children, her children, and their own child. The resulting blend of family dynamics, with four children all under the age of twelve, was causing unbearable chaos, jealousy, and fighting within their home. As if that wasn't challenging enough, their respective ex-partners were adding further complications to the situation.

Although these scenarios are very different, there is one commonality: Each parent wonders how they arrived here. What happened to the dreams they had for a warm and blissful family life? Despite their strong desires, good intentions, relentless efforts, and countless sacrifices, tension is high and joy seems scarce. The children are struggling and marriages are difficult. They can't help but wonder if there is any hope for a happier future.

Do you, too, share this sense of dissatisfaction? Has your life fallen short of the joy and fun you had envisioned and hoped for? Are you grappling with uncertainty about how to effectively guide and nurture your children? Are you disappointed in yourself, your child, or your co-parent? Do you experience guilt for not measuring up to the ideal parent you aspire to be? If you have answered yes to any of these questions, please know that you are not alone. This book is for you.

It has been my privilege to watch parents transition their homes from a place of chaos and misery to a refuge of joy and peace. What a pleasure it is to see them rediscover the delight they experienced when they first held their newborn and anticipated a bright and loving future as a family. Although their initial dreams and circumstances may have changed, they are able to discover a newfound and even deeper love in the family they are creating.

How do they do this? How might you find more peace, joy, and contentment in your home? Although there is no silver bullet, there are some simple approaches that will bring about a kinder, calmer home where all can experience joy even amid the challenges of change, growth, and development.

There are many excellent books, videos, podcasts, and other resources available to help and support parents. If you weren't so busy raising your children, you might learn from them all. However, I firmly believe that all of this wisdom and expertise can be distilled into a very simple framework of three easy to remember approaches that will allow you to parent at your best in every single circumstance.

After a lifetime of studying the research and advice of experts; parenting my own children, stepchildren, and grandchildren; and learning from the hundreds of families I have coached, it is clear to me that the keys to parenting are actually quite simple and can be applied across all generations and situations. Even my experience with parents of special needs children indicates that this framework is effective. If you would like to experience more joy and peace in your home, less guilt, and greater confidence, then read on to gain an understanding of these principles. Then enjoy real stories about how parents just like you have incorporated the framework of *Let, Lift, and Listen* into their families with amazing results.

The Three Basics of Parenting

Let, Lift, and Listen.
It's that simple. Not easy, but simple.

Let the consequences teach your children.
Lift children with honest and sincere appreciation.
Listen to your children with open ears, hearts, and minds.

This book is for parents and caregivers of children of all ages, from infants to adults. It is never too soon or too late to become the best we can be for our children.

Let, Lift, and Listen is not a new way of parenting but a summary of the most valuable parenting wisdom and advice. It is the framework through which all challenges can be approached.

Let, Lift, and Listen encompasses and summarizes time-tested parenting strategies. The approach resonates with parents because these words and tools remind us of what we instinctively comprehend about relationships but may not know how to express. By understanding and focusing on these basic truths of good parenting, with a lot of intention and a little bit of practice, you will quickly experience more joy in parenting, more peace in your home, and a better relationship with your children.

It is through my own experience, research, and personal coaching of hundreds of families that the Let, Lift, and Listen framework emerged. As a PCI Certified Parent Coach, I have been trained to co-construct effective, evidence-based strategies with the parents I serve. (Note 1.) Every family has a unique set of hopes, dreams, and values. Through my work, I have observed that certain core values appear to be universally shared. These include love, respect, honesty, kindness, and gratitude. I believe that by using the Let, Lift, and Listen framework, you will be fostering these values, and any others you identify as important, in yourselves and in your children.

An added benefit of Let, Lift, and Listen is its applicability to all age groups and relationships, both inside and outside your home. The positive impact of this approach extends beyond parenting, fostering growth and improvement in various aspects of life. Drawing from my extensive experience as a Certified Parent Coach, I have witnessed that parents who incorporate Let, Lift, and Listen into their family dynamics very quickly enjoy tremendous improvements in their marriages, friendships, and work relationships as well in as their interactions with their children.

In part 1, I provide a comprehensive overview of the three fundamental parenting approaches within the framework. In part 2, I offer further explanations and real-life examples of each element of Let, Lift, and Listen. As you immerse yourself in these authentic stories about ordinary people, you will recognize the wisdom inherent in this time-tested and proven approach to parenting. Moreover, you will discover many opportunities to apply these parenting strategies within your own family and in your own unique situation. You will want to share this book with caregivers and teachers in your children's lives so that this respectful, loving, and effective framework becomes the norm across all spheres of their upbringing.

We all know that no parenting strategy can guarantee success in raising children, yet practicing Let, Lift, and Listen ensures that you have done everything you can to cultivate joy and harmony within your home. By applying this framework, you provide your child the best possible chance to develop into a healthy, fulfilled, and valuable member of our society.

Let's get started.

PART 1
THE LET, LIFT, AND LISTEN FRAMEWORK

CHAPTER 1

Let the Consequences Do the Teaching

Imagine a mother and her children in the car, heading for a day at the beach. The cooler is packed, the beach toys are ready, and visions of the perfect family day are dancing in Mom's head. Then the inevitable happens—the kids begin to bicker in the back seat.

Without pausing to consider her response, Mom asks them to stop, repeating herself several times. The fighting continues, and she resorts to threats. "Do you want me to turn around and go home? If you don't stop this instant, we will not go to the beach. I mean it!"

The exchange goes on for a few minutes. Her anger and her voice rise, mirroring the intensity of an oncoming summer storm. The children's bickering only increases.

Now the children are angry at Mom as well as at each other. Mom is mad, disappointed, and frustrated. Her day feels ruined before she even puts her toes in the sand. Why do her children always seem to spoil her plans for a fun and joyful outing?

Now let's see what happens when Mom puts into place logical consequences and lets these consequences do the teaching instead of her harsh voice and threats.

When the bickering begins, Mom remains calm and quiet as she puts her foot on the brake, beginning to slow down—*way down*—and moving into the right lane. All of a sudden, the kids in the back stop arguing. There is silence for a moment until one of them speaks up. "Hey, Mom, what are you doing? Traffic is backing up behind us! Why are you going so slow?"

Mom calmly responds, "Oh, I'm sorry. I have a hard time concentrating with all that noise coming from the back seat. I have to drive *very* slowly so I can focus."

"But, Mom, we aren't fighting anymore. *Please* go! People are honking at us."

Now Mom begins to pick up speed, and once again everything is harmonious as they all return to their joyful day. The embarrassment of stopping traffic was enough to get her children's attention, and they understand the consequences of their actions. Ultimately, the children recognize that they are in control of the driving speed. And because independence and control are what all children want, they get what they want.

Mom has just let logical consequences do the teaching. In the future, when bickering starts, she simply lifts her foot off the accelerator. (Note 2.)

REASONS FOR LETTING THE CONSEQUENCES DO THE TEACHING

"Let" is letting logical consequences do the teaching instead of yelling, threatening, lecturing, or inflicting unrelated punishments. Letting logical consequences do the teaching is preferable for several compelling reasons. If a child learns to change their behavior solely due to fear of punishment or to avoid being yelled at, they may lack the motivation to adjust their actions when parents are absent and unable to impose consequences. Additionally, this approach can inadvertently encourage the child to work harder at not getting caught rather than genuinely understanding the impact of their choices.

We are preparing our children for a life of independence in which, we hope, they will make good decisions. Logical consequences are the way the real world works. For instance, a person who drives recklessly forfeits the privilege of driving; an employee who is perpetually late for work loses their job; people who speak rudely or disrespectfully to others often find themselves alone and without friends. By implementing logical consequences, we emulate real-world dynamics, enabling our children to understand the outcomes of their actions and make better decisions.

Punishment and the use of harsh words erode the relationship between parent and child—and that relationship is crucial for parents seeking to influence the decisions their children make now and into adulthood.

WHAT DOES IT MEAN TO LET THE CONSEQUENCES DO THE TEACHING?

Connecting logical consequences to behavior can also be defined as discipline. The word *discipline* originates from the Latin word *disciplina*, which means teaching, learning, or instruction. Discipline is different from punishment, which relies on fear and shame to change behavior. The word *punish* comes from the Latin word *punier*, meaning to take vengeance or cause pain. When it comes to shaping your child's behavior, would you rather educate them or inflict pain upon them?

Research has revealed a difference in how a child's brain reacts to punishment and how it reacts to logical discipline. Punishment can lead to depression, unhappiness, anxiety, aggression, feelings of hopelessness, and the use of drugs and alcohol, as well as memory and learning difficulties. (Note 3) In contrast, teaching and instruction through discipline lead to learning.

REMOVING ANGER FROM THE DELIVERY OF CONSEQUENCES

A critical aspect of letting the consequences do the teaching is to remove anger from our delivery. (Note 4.) Instead of anger, we acknowledge and even empathize with our children's feelings. This allows the consequences to do the teaching without giving the child an opportunity to focus their emotions on us and our anger.

For example, on the way to the beach, Mom remained calm and kind. She acknowledged that her children were humiliated by her slow driving. It can be embarrassing for a teenager when traffic builds up behind their car because their mother had to slow down to concentrate on driving. In fact, it may be uncomfortable for Mom as well.

Good parents prioritize the discipline of their children so that they'll learn to behave with more maturity over any short-lived discomfort or momentary embarrassment. Like this mom, we are adults, and it is important to remind ourselves that we care more about the children in the back seat of our car than about the strangers around us.

Letting the consequences do the teaching was an approach my mom used naturally. Although she did not use the terminology I am explaining in this book, she employed the strategy like a pro. The following true story illustrates the concept brilliantly.

STORY: THE BLACK HOLE

Growing up in Wisconsin, my siblings and I drove Mom crazy with all of our stuff, especially in the winter. We would come in from sledding or walking home from school or ice-skating on the frozen lake and thoughtlessly drop everything on the floor, right inside the door. Mittens, boots, hats, coats, books, scarves, skates—you name it—piles of wet, soggy stuff were strewn across the floor.

My mom lectured, begged, threatened, and probably grew to dislike us more and more. We began to resent her and her constant nagging. My older sister thought it funny to call her Estelle the maid, and we all joined in. It was hilarious—to us.

In truth, as children we found it easier to endure Mom's nagging than to take responsibility for our belongings and put them away. Tuning out her constant reminders became second nature to us. Little did we realize the toll it took on our relationship with our hardworking and exasperated mom.

Then, as wise mothers often do, Mom outsmarted us. When my parents put an addition on our house, she designed a remarkable foyer with big doors that opened into a set of five floor-to-ceiling niches. She had allocated a dedicated space for each of us, complete with hooks for our coats, lower shelves for our boots, and reachable shelves for our books, hats, mittens, and other belongings. Little did we know that Mom was ahead of her time, pioneering the concept of cubbies way back in the 1970s. It was truly brilliant.

So what did we do when this masterpiece was complete? After Mom had labeled each of our sections and proudly shown us how easy she had made it for us? Well, if you're a parent, you can probably guess.

We dropped everything on the floor. Five kids. Five piles of wet, soggy stuff.

But Mom was a step ahead of us. She had already figured out a way to let the consequences do the teaching.

This was before the days when closet design effectively used dead corners. There was a corner cupboard for my mom and dad's coats with unused space to one side of it. To address this, the contractor had built a half wall, preventing boots and shoes from being pushed back out of sight to the bottom of the hanging closet. This created what came to be known as the black hole.

Venturing into the black hole required pushing all the coats aside and leaning over the half wall. It was dark and scary back there. Probably full of spiders.

My mom decided that since the wet belongings on the floor were in the way, she would just deposit them in the black hole, where they would be out of sight and out of mind. When we asked where our coat or scarf or bookbag was, she would sweetly reply, "Have you checked the black hole?"

We now had a choice. We could either put our things away when we arrived home, in a place that allowed them to dry and remain spider-free and easy to find, or we could lean over the wretched wall and sort through the wet, nasty pile to locate what we wanted.

We didn't like it. We complained and called her mean. However, our mother never reciprocated our anger. She refrained from delivering lectures or uttering phrases like "If you put it away . . ." Instead, she gracefully let the consequences do the teaching. Some of us learned more quickly than others. We all learned to stop complaining to her because it got us nowhere.

The black hole prompted us to reconsider our habits. The allure of an organized, spider-free storage space versus the hassle of rummaging through the black hole shifted our perspective and forced us to contemplate the benefits of responsible actions. We were left saying to ourselves, *Next time I'll put it away so that I don't have to go into the black hole.* Now that we're grown, we remember her as a smart woman instead of as a nagging mom.

AVOID RESCUING YOUR CHILD

Letting the consequences do the teaching also means that we need to refrain from rushing to rescue our children from their mistakes. In fact, making mistakes and experiencing the consequences is one of the greatest ways for our children to learn. If we protect them from ever making a mistake, we may be shielding them from experiencing failure, therefore denying them some valuable life lessons. Some parents, unable to bear witness to their children's pain, are quick to jump in and "save" them, inadvertently depriving them of invaluable opportunities to learn. Although these well-intentioned parents believe they are displaying love toward their children, and it does feel loving, they are often prioritizing their own comfort, seeking to spare themselves the pain of watching their child suffer.

STORY: JOSH FALLS INTO THE CREEK

To illustrate this, consider John and his son, Josh, who were out enjoying a day in the woods. As they were crossing a creek, Josh was jumping from stone to stone without checking to see if the stones were stable. John casually mentioned that he was carefully checking to see if the rocks were solid but refrained from lecturing or telling Josh what to do. Josh ignored his dad's wise and experienced comment and continued jumping in a carefree manner. Instead of telling him again, John decided that, because the consequences of falling in the shallow creek really weren't that severe, he would let Josh learn a consequential lesson.

Sure enough, Josh landed on a loose rock and fell into the stream. John extended a helping hand to his drenched and embarrassed son. Instead of expressing frustration or responding with "I told you to check the rocks before standing on them," John simply helped him dry off. As Josh whined about falling in, John patiently listened and empathized. As they got ready to cross the creek again, John noticed Josh tentatively checking each rock before carefully placing his foot on it. What could have been a negative interaction between father and son allowed the outing to continue in a friendly way. Moreover, John noticed with satisfaction that Josh had indeed learned a lesson. Perhaps, as a secondary lesson, Josh also discovered that Dad offers good advice!

WHEN YOU OR YOUR CHILD ARE EMBARRASSED

Embarrassment often comes into play when parents embrace the approach of letting the consequences do the teaching. We feel pain when our child is embarrassed. Although it is always important to refrain from intentionally embarrassing our children, when embarrassment is a result of their own behavior or decisions, it can serve as a natural consequence. In such situations we can offer unwavering empathy and support.

And *we* don't want to be embarrassed by our child's misbehavior. However, if a parent succumbs to their own embarrassment and intervenes to rescue their child, they may actually be loving themselves more than their child as they unknowingly steal an opportunity for their child to learn.

STORY: LOUISA FORGETS HER HOMEWORK

Louisa is perpetually forgetting her homework and gets very upset when her teacher makes her stay in from recess to complete it. If Mom or Dad regularly take the homework to school so that Louisa doesn't miss recess or so that they look like a better parent, they are stealing a valuable opportunity from the child to learn and grow.

Mom might think she is offering consequences by delivering the homework and then lecturing or punishing later when in reality, she is rescuing Louisa from natural consequences as she tunes out Mom's well-meaning lectures.

A more effective response to Louisa might be the following:

> Louisa (voice quivering): "I missed recess today and had to stay in to do my homework. And I had already done it. Why wouldn't you bring it to me? You're so mean."

> Mom: "Oh Louisa, I know how you hate to miss recess. That's horrible. And you had to stay in from recess and do the same work you did last night? How frustrating."

> Louisa: "Why wouldn't you bring my homework to me?"

> Mom: "Well, Louisa, I had a busy day myself."

> Louisa: "You're so mean!"

Mom: "It probably feels that way. And I love you. Shall we go to the park now, since you didn't get to run and play today?"

It is a real gift when someone else, such as the teacher in this case, imposes the consequences. It makes it very easy for the parent to remain compassionate. Notice that Mom never got angry at Louisa. Why should she? Louisa's learning opportunity did not affect Mom at all. In fact, she knew her daughter needed to get out and play, and she even took her to the park.

An observant mother might recognize that Louisa may need to develop some habits to help her remember things. Perhaps she'll make some suggestions that evening such as "Would you like to put your homework in your backpack now so that you'll have it when your teacher asks tomorrow?"

Using the approach of letting logical consequences happen has provided Louisa with a real-life incentive to learn to remember to take her homework to school and turn it in. At the same time, her relationship with her mother is being built by her compassionate responses to Louisa's complaints.

Parenting Tip: When You Disagree with Another Caregiver

In this story about Louisa, Mom may think the teacher was wrong to keep her child from recess. She may, in fact, decide to make efforts for the school to implement different consequences that do not withhold needed exercise. However, it is not appropriate to agree with or suggest to the child that the teacher was wrong. You are preparing your child for the real world where others are not always fair or do things the way you might. The child is paying consequences that are actually quite minor.

Joining forces with your child against another person shifts the focus away from the child's behavior. For example, if Louisa's mom agrees that taking recess away was mean, Louisa is no longer thinking about the fact that she did not complete her homework; instead, she is thinking about the mean teacher.

It is not uncommon for parents to disagree with each other about consequences. What if the other parent reacts to a situation with words or consequences that you disagree with? Unless there is serious harm involved, your opinion should only be expressed out of earshot of your child. Adjusting the consequences as a result of a child complaining can hurt relationships between the child and the more restrictive parent and can lead to conflict and anger between the parents. When parents disagree about consequences, this should always be dealt with away from the child and presented as a unified decision.

Certainly, there may be times when your child has been unfairly treated by an adult, and it is important to listen carefully, offer empathy, and help the child determine an appropriate response. By actively listening and refraining from placing blame on either the child or another adult, we keep the lines of communication open. Listening, of course, is especially important in the event there is serious wrongdoing by the adult.

Letting natural consequences do the teaching is, without question, the most effective approach to helping our children develop life skills, habits, and behaviors that will serve them and the world around them in a positive way. As parents, we often have to get creative as we determine what a good natural consequence might be. A crucial aspect is to tie the consequence, in a meaningful way, directly to the behavior we're trying to correct. Wrapping our words and reactions in sincere love and empathy maintains the vital connection between us and our children. For parents seeking further information and examples, I highly recommend reading *Parenting with Love and Logic* by Foster Cline and Jim Fay. (See the resources list at the end of the book.)

APPLICATION

Consider: What is a behavior in your child that needed correction during the past week? Did you implement a logical consequence or a punishment for the infraction?

If you resorted to lecturing or punishing, can you think of a more logical consequence?

Did you offer empathy and compassion to the child for the consequence they had to endure?

If you're feeling guilty about the way you handled the situation, don't fret. Our children are generous in giving us many opportunities to try again!

Consider: Was there a situation this past week where your child could have learned a valuable lesson through a natural consequence if you hadn't intervened to warn or rescue them?

Consider: In the story, "Josh Falls into the Creek", John reaches out and helps Josh out of the creek and helps him dry off. Is this rescuing him? Why or why not?

Practice: What are some possible natural consequences for the following scenarios? Refer to part 2 for ideas regarding these and other situations.

> ➤ Your child consistently sleeps late in the morning, misses the bus, and needs a ride to school.

> ➤ Your child told you that her room was cleaned up and then headed next door to play with her friends. You discover the room is still a mess.
> ➤ Your child informed you that he would be studying at a friend's house, but you spot him hanging out at the park with his buddies.

KEY POINTS

> ➤ All consequences should be logically linked to the child's behavior.
> ➤ Responding to challenging behavior with empathy helps maintain the connection between parent and child while also keeping the child's focus on themselves rather than on the parent.
> ➤ Allowing your child to experience the discomfort of logical consequences is more loving than rescuing them, which would only relieve our pain or discomfort.

CHAPTER 2

Lift Your Children with Honest Appreciation

Consider sixteen-year-old Chandler, who gets into frequent fights at school. Because of this ongoing behavior, he has been expelled. A typical parent reaction might be to yell at, punish, and make him realize how stupid or bad he is. It would not be unreasonable for a frustrated parent to launch into a tirade like this:

> "Why would you do such a stupid thing? You knew you would get in big trouble! Now you've been kicked out of school. This infuriates me. Don't you ever learn? What is wrong with you? That's it. You're going to military school. See how you like that. That will teach you a lesson."

Would it be possible in this situation to "lift" a child and offer sincere appreciation for a strength the child has shown in such a difficult circumstance? I know a dad who offered this reaction:

> Dad (taking a deep breath with a very sad look): "Whoa, this is really sad. What happened, Chandler?"

Chandler: "I had enough. The guy is a bully, and I was sick and tired of him. He's mean to everyone, and he called me a wimp. I knew I shouldn't have hit him, but he deserved it."

Dad: "You know, son, you've always stood up for yourself and others. You possess a real sense of justice. I remember when you were very young, and you went after that boy who was being mean to your little sister. Being a person who stands up for what is right is not a bad thing. In fact, our world needs more of that. A sense of justice will take you a long way in life. Unfortunately, fighting is not the way to stand up for justice, and I'm so sorry you have to go away to military school. We're really going to miss you."

In both examples, whether it's the tirade or the gentler approach, the consequence for Chandler remains the same: Chandler is going to military school.

However, Chandler would likely respond to these reactions in different ways.

In the first example, the father resorted to shaming and punishing his son, lacking any expression of compassion. As a result, Chandler would probably feel a sense of inadequacy and likely direct his emotions toward his father and how terrible he is to send him to military school. This would divert his attention from reflecting on his own behavior.

In the second example, Chandler would likely understand that the serious consequence was a result of his own actions. He would be reminded, by the one who knows him best, that he really does have what it takes, deep down inside and within his character. The inner voice he would carry the rest of his life would likely consist of phrases such as *I have what it takes, I'm a person of justice, I'm needed in this world, I'm going to make it, my dad loves me* instead of harboring thoughts like *I'm bad, I'm hopeless, I'm a problem, even my own dad doesn't want me around.*

Even when faced with a very bad situation, we can usually discover something about our child that deserves genuine praise. This gives our children hope and reassurance that they can overcome obstacles.

This approach represents the second strategy: *lift*. Effective parents lift their children through honest and sincere praise.

Children are desperate to know, and to prove, that they have what it takes, that they are going to make it, and that they will succeed in life. By acknowledging and remembering their strengths, we communicate to them that they do indeed possess the abilities needed not only for daily tasks but also for life as a whole.

WHAT IS LIFTING?

"Lifting" is not flattery. Flattery is typically insincere, lacking specificity, and often exaggerated, such as saying "You're the greatest kid!" or even making untrue claims like "You're the best soccer player in the whole wide world!" Genuine praise, on the other hand, sounds like this: "You make me smile when you play so nicely with your little sister" or "The determination you showed today while chasing the ball was truly impressive. You never gave up. You have such a go-getter attitude!"

A good rule of thumb is to lift your child five times for every correction you offer. Extensive research in the field of problem-solving has demonstrated that instead of focusing 80 percent on what is not working and 20 percent on strengths, reversing the tendency (80 percent positive to 20 percent negative) resulted in radical change. (Note 5.) This general finding is consistent with empirical evidence in over a dozen other scientific studies on realizing our higher potential. (Note 6.)

Achieving this 5:1 ratio can be challenging, especially during the adolescent years. Teenagers do really dumb things sometimes (refer to the parenting tip on brain development in chapter 8), and it can be hard to see the positives in the mistakes they make. However, parents who cultivate this 5:1 habit when their children are young find it more natural and easier to maintain as their children mature.

STORY: SLOWPOKE, SLOWPOKE

I once saw a mom taking her toddler to the beach. Poor Mom was lugging a cooler, buckets of toys, a sun umbrella, and a beach bag full of sunscreen, towels, and even a book she probably would not get to read. Meanwhile, her toddler was stopping to investigate every stone and bug along the way. The well-meaning mom sweetly sang out, "Slowpoke, slowpoke, you are such a slowpoke" while kindly urging her child to pick up the pace. However, it raises the question of what message she is embedding in her child's mind. What seeds might she have sown if, instead, she had remarked, "You're always so curious. Mommy is having trouble carrying all these things. Please try to move a little faster"?

Parenting Tip: Use _and_ Instead of _but_

Many parents fall into the habit of using the word "but" when trying to affirm their children. Unfortunately, when "but" is used to connect two phrases in a sentence, it essentially dismisses or negates the importance of the first phrase. In contrast, the word "and" allows the parent to lift their child even when there is more to be done.

For example, instead of saying, "Nice job in math, _but_ what happened in English?" Try saying, "Wow, nice job in math, _and_ English is more of a struggle."

Instead of saying, "You did a great job getting up on your own this morning, _but_ your hair is a mess," try saying, "Wow, you got up on your own this morning, brushed your teeth, got dressed, _and_ now all you have left is to brush your hair."

Using the word "and" instead of "but" also communicates agreement and promotes collaboration.

For example, instead of saying, "I know you're tired, _but_ you still need to clean your room," try saying, "I know you're tired, _and_ you still need to clean your room."

Instead of saying, "I know you want to watch TV, _but_ you still need to finish your homework," try saying, "I know you want to watch TV, _and_ you need to finish your homework."

Instead of saying, "I know you really want that new toy, but it's a long time until your birthday," try saying, "I know you really want that new toy, _and_ we'll look at it again closer to your birthday."

But	And
Excludes or is _dismissive_ of that which precedes it	Expands and includes what precedes it
Negates, discounts, or cancels that which precedes it	Acknowledges what precedes it
May easily be perceived as pejorative	Perceived as more neutral
Suggests the first issue is subordinate to the second	Suggests there are two issues to be addressed

WHY LIFTING IS IMPORTANT

Most children act with confidence, especially in their teen years. Although they make it clear that they know what is best for themselves, the truth is that they're afraid. They're afraid they may disappoint us, afraid they're not going to be liked by their friends, and afraid they don't have what it takes to navigate life independently. If their own parents, who know them better than anyone else, do not believe in their capabilities, how can they believe in themselves?

What they truly need from us is to remember, notice, and state what is true about them, deep inside. We are giving them a vision of their future, and it needs to be a good one. When you have a sullen, smelly, teenage boy lying on your couch refusing to do his chores or homework, remember that residing inside that teenage body is the same little boy who used to make heartfelt valentines and who was always underfoot wanting to help so that he could receive more of those hugs and kisses from you that melted your heart.

IT'S NEVER TOO LATE

Are you feeling guilty or sad for believing that you haven't lifted your children as well as you might have? Or maybe you think you were too hard on your child? Join the club. You're not alone. Every parent, including myself, experiences these feelings. No one gets it right all the time, and only very few manage to get it right most of the time. The good news is that our children are resilient. And if they *never* experienced criticism as children, they might not know how to handle it when they're out in the real world.

Never forget: Your voice will *always* be powerful. You will always have opportunities to lift your children at any age. You have the ability to lift them in life-changing ways. It's never too late to start being more intentional about lifting your children as well as everyone else in your life, starting this very moment.

APPLICATION

Consider: What interior voices are you speaking into your child's mind? What voices do you want to speak?

Consider: Thinking of a recent situation where your child demonstrated a need for correction, what strength was being exhibited at the same time? Was it boldness? Perseverance? Persuasion?

Practice: Make a list of your child's strengths. Think back to who they were as a young child. Add to and review the list every day for a week. As you consistently practice lifting your child, you may discover that it becomes easier to recall the traits from the list so that you more naturally notice and remark on these strengths in your child, even in the midst of challenging behavior.

Practice: Make a list of your own strengths, as a parent, a friend, a coworker. Lean into these strengths as you focus on becoming the best parent you can be.

Practice: Read the following examples and fill in the blanks.

Negative Interior Voice	Lifting Voice
You only care about your Xbox and games.	You work so hard on those games and are persistent.
You are so lazy. You never do your chores.	You really know how to relax. You are good at choosing what you want to do.
You choose bad friends.	You choose exciting friends.
You never stop talking.	You are full of ideas.

You don't sit still.	You are full of energy.
You are only concerned about your appearance.	
You are always on your telephone.	
You stay up too late at night.	
You talk about other people too much.	
You are too bossy.	

Practice: At the end of the calendar or school year, take the time to write a heartfelt letter to each of your children, highlighting their accomplishments throughout that period. Do your best to avoid listing or focusing on achievements such as grades or championships and instead make an effort to emphasize character traits like perseverance, hard work, and positive attitudes.

KEY POINTS

➢ Children long to know that their parents believe the best in them.

➢ The words parents use during their children's early years can have a lasting impact, becoming internalized voices throughout their lifetimes.

➢ Noticing strengths in the midst of challenges does not undermine the importance of imposing logical consequences.

➢ Using the word *and* promotes inclusivity, kindness, and collaboration.

CHAPTER 3

Listen to Your Children with Open Ears, Hearts, and Minds

Mom is taken aback, as well as slightly amused, as her seventh grader, Matt, confidently declares, "I've decided to drop out of school, practice basketball all the time, and become an NBA player."

Mom knows it's ridiculous. To begin with, Matt is not very tall, and with parents both under five nine, the chances of becoming an NBA superstar are slim. And, of course, she understands the importance of education and is not going to let him drop out of school. There are legal implications as well as practical reasons why Matt's idea is not a good one.

Despite her initial urge to interrupt and explain the implausibility of Matt's plan, Mom remembers the importance of listening with an open mind, heart, and ears. She has come to understand that listening does not mean she agrees. And she is always looking for ways to lift and encourage her child. Imagine the conversation progressing like this:

Mom: "Wow. I must say, you're truly talented at basketball, and you understand the value of practice. I can see how quitting school would certainly give you plenty of time to practice. Please, tell me more."

Matt: "Yeah, Mom! If I didn't have to waste my whole day at stupid school, I could practice so much more and become really amazing. And you know how much NBA players make? I could buy us all a new house! And we could go on incredible vacations! Plus, imagine seeing me on TV. It would be great. I just need more time to devote to practice."

As Mom attentively listens, she becomes curious and decides to ask a few questions. She genuinely wants to understand Matt better—his goals, what he doesn't like about school, and what he might do with potential wealth. Through this conversation, she hopes to find opportunities to lift him by acknowledging his ambition, enthusiasm, generosity, and physical skill.

Matt is enjoying this conversation and feels very respected by his mom. He senses that she genuinely values his perspective and desires. Deep down, Matt might already realize that quitting school is not a practical option. By allowing him to state this to himself instead of hearing his mom tell him, he has less reason to argue. Ideas hold more power when they originate from within oneself.

In addition to honest questions such as "How did you come up with this idea?" Mom could pose other questions or make a few statements that allow him to process the reality of his plan. For example, she could ask, "I wonder if it's legal for a seventh grader to quit school?" or "Could you remain on your school team if you weren't a student?"

Instead of ending the conversation with advice, Mom could offer words of encouragement: "You certainly have some ambitions ideas. It'll be fascinating to see what you do in life."

With this kind of positive communication, her son might decide to put in extra effort and practice harder after school. Or the idea might naturally fade away, leading him to develop other creative ideas as he is encouraged to continue thinking and dreaming. Sometimes working through an outrageous dream is what helps a person firmly plant their feet on the ground again. (Note 7.) Regardless of where the conversation leads, rather than shutting down her child, Mom has nurtured excitement and creativity in her son.

THE BENEFITS OF GOOD LISTENING

Listening with open ears, hearts, and minds is an incredibly powerful tool for parents. Business research has shown that effective listening yields numerous benefits. By truly listening, you gain more information from the people you interact with, build trust, reduce conflict, gain insight into how to motivate others, and inspire a higher level of commitment from those you manage. (Note 8.) As the "manager" of your own household, wouldn't you love these same results by enhancing your listening skills?

It's common for most parents to believe that they're good listeners. After all, it seems like a simple task and a normal part of everyday conversation—one person talks while the other listens, and vice versa. However, a study involving more than eight thousand individuals in the business field revealed that virtually all the respondents believed that they communicate as effectively or more effectively than others. (Note 9.) This finding raises a question: can everyone truly be above average in their listening skills? Additionally, research indicates that the average person listens with only about 25 percent efficiency. (Note 10.)

HOW TO LISTEN EFFECTIVELY

To listen effectively requires deliberate thought and purpose. But what does it mean to listen effectively? The concept has been defined as actively absorbing the information given to you by a speaker, showing that you are listening and interested, and providing feedback to the speaker so that they know the message was received. Effective listeners show speakers that they have been heard and understood. (Note 11.)

It appears to me, from my own experience as a parent and a coach, that many parents listen even less effectively to their children than to other adults. Why is this? Perhaps it is because we have a strong desire to impart our hard-earned wisdom. We genuinely believe that if they would just listen to us, we could spare them from experiencing the pain of learning through their own mistakes.

With so much more life experience than our children, we often find ourselves lecturing our kids. Naturally, we do this out of love and concern for them. So instead of truly *listening* to their perspectives, we tend to *tell* them what to do and even what to think. When they don't respond, we tell them again—and again and again. However, if we're spending the whole time telling instead of listening, we fail to provide them with the attention and respect they desperately need for their own ideas to flourish.

Allowing our children to express their opinions is very important. It not only models respect but also allows us to discover new aspects of their personalities and thoughts. By giving them space to wrestle through their own ideas, they may even arrive at the same conclusions we would have. Moreover, when we listen well, it helps our children develop the ability to listen to others, including us!

Parenting Tip: Listening Does Not Mean We Agree

In the aforementioned scenario, Matt's mom did not agree with Matt's plan. However, she knew that sincerely listening did not imply automatic agreement. It is crucial for us to grasp the concept that we can attentively listen to and comprehend anyone's viewpoint while still expressing our disagreement if we choose to do so. Allowing our children to elaborate and clearly express their thoughts, ideas, and opinions does not imply that we support or endorse their thoughts or plans. As parents, we still retain the authority to set rules within our homes. Effective listening doesn't alter this fact.

You can try incorporating phrases such as these: "Hmm, I never thought about it that way. Tell me more." "That might not be the approach I would take, but I'm not you. Tell me more."

By using such words, we create an atmosphere where our children feel heard and respected, even if we don't ultimately agree with their viewpoints.

What if your child is telling you something requiring a response that you know is going to make her angry?

For instance, let's say your fourteen-year-old daughter, Rachel, announces that she is quitting volleyball because her coach is so mean. You might instinctively want to respond by listing all the reasons she shouldn't quit: the season has already been paid for, the importance of teamwork, the value of physical fitness, and not letting her team down. Taking this approach could easily turn the conversation into a lecture and eventually lead to an argument, leaving Rachel feeling unheard and misunderstood.

Besides, you're not even sure why she wants to quit because she always seemed to like her coach. Is it because she didn't make the top team?

Is she being reprimanded for being too social? Would she rather be hanging out with her new crush? Worse yet, could there be any form of abuse happening? Although you may think you understand her motivation, do you really? Wouldn't it be helpful to find out?

Let's explore how the conversation might unfold if you really focus on the importance of listening. Effective listening often begins with repeating, restating, or reflecting back what you believe the other person said.

> Mom: "Hmm, sounds like you're not enjoying volleyball."
>
> Rachel (exasperated): "It's not volleyball! I love volleyball. It's my stupid coach."
>
> Mom (gentle tone): "Of course. You've always loved volleyball. That's why you've worked so hard at it and have even given up other things so that you could play. I think I hear you. Your coach is stupid? She doesn't understand volleyball?"
>
> Rachel: "No. She doesn't understand me. She's mean and stupid. And she made me sit out for half of practice today."

(Notice how restating what you believe you heard leads to further clarification.)

> Mom: "That's awful. I agree. It's no fun to be around someone who is mean and stupid. Sitting on the sidelines is also not fun. Please, tell me more."

Rachel: "She's always yelling at me and Sonya for talking. But the truth is we're talking about volleyball! Sonya knows more about it than our coach."

Mom: "So she doesn't like it when you and Sonya are talking, even when it's about volleyball?"

Rachel: "Right. That's why I want to quit."

Mom: "I don't blame you for feeling that way. You've always enjoyed volleyball, and now it's not as much fun for you. I'm not in your shoes, and I may be totally wrong, but if I were you, I would be mighty sad about missing the big tournament in Orlando in April."

Rachel: "I know. I want to quit, but I don't want to quit."

Mom: "I hear you."

Instead of blowing up into an argument, by listening so intently and without judgment, the conversation has led to a deeper understanding and connection between your daughter and you. Rachel now feels loved and understood, and you have gained more insight into what's happening in her life. Whether she decides to quit volleyball or not, and whether you permit it or not, is a separate matter.

Regardless of the outcome, the conversation has drawn you closer together. Parents who remain aware of and practice good listening skills in such moments are more likely to maintain a positive relationship with their children.

But what should you do if your child insists on an immediate response? What if Rachel pushes for an answer, repeatedly asking her mom if she can quit? How might a parent respond? One approach might be to say, "Honey, I hear that you're unhappy. Considering the number of years you've played, I think we should take more time before making such a big decision. Let's discuss it again next week."

Note that this is not a promise to allow her to quit. It's an honest and sincere agreement to consider Rachel's desire. There are so many possible outcomes: Rachel may change her mind, Mom may allow her to quit, or Mom may insist that she finish the season. Pressing the pause button does not exclude any of these possible outcomes. If a child demands an immediate response, a parent might say, "If you want a response right now, you might not like it."

LISTENING TO EMOTIONS

A deeper and equally powerful way of listening entails paying attention to your child's emotions. All children experience big emotions, but they are not naturally equipped to identify what they are feeling, why they feel that way, and how to handle those emotions. They desperately need adults to assist them in developing these skills. To really listen to your child can be like acting as a detective as you uncover and understand your child's emotions. Your child needs your guidance in learning to identify their emotions and the most constructive ways to manage them.

STORY: MARIO THROWS HIS BOOKBAG

Imagine that your child, Mario, walks in the front door, throws down his bookbag in the middle of the floor, and heads straight to his room. You've told him countless times to put his bag in his cubby and to say hello when he walks in. You interpret his behavior as rude and disrespectful and respond by either yelling at him or applying what seems to you a logical consequence.

However, what you (like many parents) may have missed is the opportunity to learn more about what might be going on with your child. Perhaps someone on the bus called him a hurtful name, and he doesn't want you to see him cry. Maybe he flunked his math test and fears your disappointment or anger. It's even possible he's worried about his hamster because he forgot to feed it that morning. Perhaps you have no idea of what's going on!

By taking the time to delve deeper and listen to your child's emotions, you can forge a stronger connection. Instead of solely focusing on your child's behavior, you can empathetically inquire about their feelings and concerns, creating an environment where your child feels safe to express himself. This approach opens up the opportunity for understanding and support, allowing you to provide the guidance your child needs in navigating his emotions effectively.

There is real power in pausing prior to responding (see the parenting tip on the power of the pause in chapter 7). Pausing not only allows you to carefully consider your reply but also leaves space for your child to continue expressing himself.

Let's return to the story about Mario and his bad attitude as he threw his bookbag on the floor. A parent genuinely committed to listening might pause, identify their own emotions (I'm irritated with my child), and then approach the child with love and empathy. Let's assume, in this example, that Mario was worried about his hamster.

You knock on his door and find him feeding Sir Ham. You watch, silently, as your child tells you he was scared because he forgot to feed Sir Ham. Relieved that this is all that was going on, you lift him by commenting on how lucky Sir Ham is to have such a responsible owner who cares so much. You also mention that it explains why he threw his backpack in the middle of the floor, since, lately, he's been so diligent about putting it away. In this case, your child has correctly identified his emotion (worry), and you have provided him the space and permission to do so.

But what if the reason he threw his backpack in the middle of the floor was that someone called him a name on the bus ride home from school? When you knock on his door, he tells you to get lost.

Now you're more than just irritated; you're feeling angry because of his rudeness. Having acquired the ability to regulate your own emotions, you walk away and fix a cup of tea to compose yourself. Later, when you're both calm, you might spend some time together helping him understand his emotions. (Anger? Embarrassment? Sadness?) You can also help him brainstorm effective ways to handle his emotions without being rude to others.

Many of us are quick to react to behaviors without attempting to understand or help our children comprehend their emotions or the emotions of others. When we raise our children in this way, we risk sending them out into the world without the ability to effectively respond to their own emotions or to empathize with the emotions of others. It serves our family and our society well when we become proficient in these emotional skills. For further information on effectively acquiring these skills, I recommend Marc Brackett's book *Permission to Feel* (see the resources list at the end of the book).

REFLECT ON EVENTS

During stressful situations, our own emotional turmoil can hinder our ability to perceive and comprehend our children's actions clearly. When we attain a state of emotional calmness, we enhance our capacity to think logically, improve our listening skills, and become better equipped to support our children. It can also be helpful to discuss the situation with another person who knows and loves our child, reflecting on the factors that might have prompted our child to act in a certain way.

BODY LANGUAGE AND ATTENTIVENESS

Being totally attentive to your child when they talk is kind, respectful, and loving. If you find yourself too occupied to pause what you're doing and give your child your full attention, kindly inform them that you want to hear what they have to say and that they need to wait momentarily. Be sure to follow up with them as soon as possible.

When you do listen, give your full presence. Lower yourself to eye level when communicating with young children. It is usually best to face your child directly and establish eye contact. The only exception might be when having difficult discussions with your teenager. Sometimes conversations with older children are easier to navigate when sitting side by side and looking forward.

Reflecting on my early years as a busy mother, I sadly recall attempting to juggle multiple tasks at once, especially listening and responding to my children. I would offer half-hearted replies like *hmm, uh-huh,* and *that's interesting* without truly paying attention. One day my son called me out on this, stamping his little foot and saying, "Mommy, you are not *listening* to me." He was absolutely right, and his words hit me hard. I felt awful but grateful for the opportunities he continued to provide me to become a better listener.

The truth is, we cannot effectively multitask while listening attentively to others. (Note 12.) We miss out on what is being shared at the same time we are communicating a lack of respect and concern for the person speaking.

In today's world, our smartphones often contribute a lack of attentiveness to our children and others. Consider what you are communicating to your child every time you choose to look at your phone while they are talking to you. Are you sending the message that you prioritize your phone over your child? Wise parents ignore their phone during conversations with family members. They might also require everyone to turn off their phone notifications during mealtimes. This type of behavior emphasizes and models the importance of human connection.

CHILDREN WHO DON'T COMMUNICATE

No doubt, some of you may be thinking, *That advice is all well and good for parents whose children talk to them. My young child never stops talking; it's my teenager who rarely communicates with me, except for the occasional grunt or request for money.*

There is no way to make your child talk to you. However, besides attentive listening, there is an additional approach that is respectful, loving, and encouraging—door openers, a commonly used term in the field of communication. A door opener typically takes the form of a statement, although it can also be an open-ended and nonspecific question. It serves as an inviting and noncoercive gesture, rather than as a demand, extended to your child—a way to open the door to conversation. Such a statement conveys your understanding of what the other person might be thinking, doing, or feeling.

Here are some examples of door openers:

> ➢ You appear to be troubled.
> ➢ You sure look excited.
> ➢ You seem quite annoyed.
> ➢ You appear upset about something.

> ➤ It seems like things really went well. Can you tell me more about it?
> ➤ That's an interesting idea. I'd love to hear more.

Many of us believe that being a good listener means asking a lot of questions. However, others, especially teenagers, perceive a lot of specific questions as an interrogation. Asking many questions can be seen as a subtle way of exerting control over a conversation.

From a very young age, children strive for independence and a sense of control. They want to be in control. When they feel that we are taking control of conversations by bombarding them with questions, they often shut down. They dislike feeling dominated in the conversation, so they choose to stop talking or, worse, become irritated. Instead of relying heavily on questions, consider using door openers to foster communication.

STORY: TAMIKA AND HER MATH TEST

Tamika has been studying very hard for a math test. She is stressed out by the upcoming exam, and her mom has been helping her study and providing support. On the day of the big test, Mom picks Tamika up at school and greets her with a question: "How was the exam?"

This seems appropriate and considerate, right? Mom is demonstrating her care and is in tune with Tamika's day. However, it is entirely possible that Tamika doesn't want to discuss it yet. Perhaps it went poorly, and she simply doesn't feel like talking about it. Perhaps she doesn't want to disappoint or upset her mom. Alternatively, even if the test went smoothly, there might be something else that happened at school that is occupying Tamika's thoughts.

In this situation, using a door opener instead of a direct question could sound like this:

> Mom: "Hi, Tamika."
>
> (Moment of silence to give Tamika a chance to share if she wishes.)
>
> Tamika remains silent.
>
> Mom (door opener): "You had that big exam today."

By mentioning the exam without pressing for an immediate response, Tamika now has the freedom to speak or remain silent, based on her own choice. The mention of the exam lets her know that Mom is present and available. She understands that her mom cares about her and is in tune with her day. Attempting to make Tamika talk by bombarding her with questions could potentially lead to an argument (at worst) or an irritated daughter (at best). There is no way a parent can force a child to talk; they can only offer the love and respect that children desperately need while creating an open door to conversation.

Effective communication is vital in our role as parents or caregivers. It's important to keep in mind that *listening does not mean we agree*. Being fully present and attentive is a kind and respectful approach. Moreover, it's essential to avoid bombarding our children with excessive questions, as it can come across as an interrogation, hindering effective communication. By practicing these principles, you will move toward happier and more effective parenting.

Fortunately, there are a wealth of resources available to enhance our communication skills. I encourage you to grow and learn in this area. One highly recommended book for parents is *How to Talk So Kids will*

Listen and Listen So Kids will Talk by Adele Faber and Elaine Mazlish (see the resources list at the end of the book). This classic book provides valuable insights and strategies for improving parent-child communication.

APPLICATION

Consider: We all expect our children to pay attention, listen, and respond respectfully when we are speaking to them. Are you modeling this behavior when your child speaks to you?

Consider: Are you giving your child permission to feel? Are you providing a safe space for them to express their emotions? Or are you jumping to conclusions about what they're feeling and why?

Practice: Make a conscious effort to use door openers more often than relying on questions. In the following examples, replace the questions with suitable door openers.

Question: How was your day?

Door opener: *Welcome home. I would love to hear about your day.*

Question: What are you going to do over your summer vacation?

Door opener: *Wow. School is out in one week. You have the whole summer ahead of you.*

Question: Are you angry about something?

Door opener: *I notice that you look upset.*

Question: How was your history test?

Door opener: _____

Question: What did you do at your friend's house?

Door opener: _____

Question: Did you have fun at the park?

Door opener: _____

Question: How was your first day at your new job?

Door opener: _____

KEY POINTS

- ➤ Listening does not imply agreement.
- ➤ The power of the pause is tremendous.
- ➤ Attentive listening models respect and kindness.
- ➤ When given the opportunity, people, including children, can often work through their own dilemmas.
- ➤ Using door-opening statements honors a child's autonomy and encourages a child to express themselves more freely.

CHAPTER 4

Love: The Foundation of Let, Lift, and Listen

I f Let, Lift, and Listen serve as the guiding framework of good parenting, love is the solid foundation. Every action, every word, every thought, when grounded in love, has exponential power to help you guide your child. As they mature, your control over them will diminish, but your influence will likely increase. This influence is earned by laying and maintaining a foundation of love. Unconditional love.

With intentionality, and with practice, effective parents undergird and wrap every bit of the framework of Let, Lift, and Listen in an atmosphere of love and compassion.

The notion of reminding parents to love their children may appear superfluous. At times, we may find ourselves not particularly fond of our children; we might experience frustration, anger, and embarrassment or even wonder why we ever thought having children was a good idea. At the same time, most parents possess a profound, innate, and unwavering love for their children.

Why do we often experience stronger anger toward our own children when they misbehave compared to a child from the neighborhood who commits the same mistake? It is frequently our deep love for our own children that intensifies our anger and frustration. We genuinely care about our children, which is why their behavior, if it may lead to unfavorable outcomes, deeply upsets us. Being angry doesn't *feel* like love. It is very complex.

When we understand that our intense emotions can stem from our love for our children, we are then capable of maintaining a calm and compassionate demeanor, even during challenging moments.

Love is not always a feeling. In fact, Erich Fromm, a social psychologist, psychoanalyst, and German philosopher, enlightens us in his book *The Art of Loving* that love is active, not passive. (Note 13.)

We don't lecture because we like to lecture; we lecture because we love our children deeply and because we genuinely want what is best for them. We don't discipline our children because we like to discipline but rather because we love and care about them. We don't sit back and let them learn from their mistakes because we derive pleasure from their pain but because our love for them compels us to prioritize their growth and the acquisition of important life lessons. We love our children.

Sadly, our actions often defy our truest feelings. An angry face does not look like love. Endless lectures convey a sense of disdain and a lack of confidence in our child. When discipline is delivered as a form of punishment, it inflicts pain. As parents, our challenge lies in effectively communicating this unstoppable love while also endeavoring to guide and shape our child's behavior.

So how can we communicate unconditional and unstoppable love to our children when we ourselves feel scared, frustrated, or angry? It's not easy. However, once you manage to do so, you will experience a surprising joy that exceeds your expectations. And it gets easier with time.

EXPRESSING LOVE AMID CHALLENGES

The first step is to pause. Take a few deep breaths. Go for a walk or a run. Grant yourself the time, space, and compassion to feel what you feel. This not only might prevent you from uttering regrettable words but also might give you time to reconnect with the deep love you have for your child. Moreover, you will be modeling to your children a mature approach to managing big emotions.

Children are not like your family pet, who requires immediate consequences. Kids older than toddlers seldom forget what they have done to elicit a negative response from you. If you are in a calm enough frame of mind, stating that you are too upset to talk about it now gives your child time to reflect on what has happened.

Responding to your child with empathy is powerful. If you can make the first words or sounds coming out of your mouth those of empathy, you immediately communicate love. It conveys the message that you genuinely care about them and that you are on the same team. At the same time, it communicates that this is a problem for the child, not the parent. Using empathetic language, such as the following, is the best way to begin your response to any challenge you encounter with your children:

➢ "I'm so sad for you."
➢ "Oh no. This is not going to work out well."
➢ "We'll miss you when you're in your room/at military school/ in jail."

> ➤ "Uh-oh."
> ➤ "That must be really hard."

Including hugs and soft expressions enhances the message of love.

We can behave with empathy and sadness because these are genuine emotions experienced by most parents. Beneath our anger lies sadness. We *would* be happier if our child were playing nicely with everyone else instead of alone in their room. We *would* be happier for our child if she had been studying in the library so that she wouldn't flunk her classes or lose some privileges. Underneath our frustration and anger *is* love. Understanding these truths enables us to truly express compassion and love.

WHY EXPRESS LOVE INSTEAD OF ANGER?

We let consequences do the teaching in an atmosphere of love because it encourages the child to reflect on their own behavior rather than focusing on ours. Another reason for expressing love instead of anger is that it diminishes the child's inclination to direct their anger toward you, allowing their energy to be channeled toward self-reflection. Instead of thinking, *I'm mad at my mom or dad for taking my privileges/car away,* they are more likely to think, *I'm mad at myself for coming home late last night.*

We lift in an atmosphere of love by actively seeking opportunities to communicate our love for and belief in our child, even when they have made mistakes. This reassures the child and reminds the parent that we see, believe in, and love them for who they are, even in the face of poor decisions and consequences. Love for our child is not the same as approval for what they are doing.

We listen in an atmosphere of love by genuinely hearing and respecting our children. We express love by validating their thoughts and feelings. Although we may not always agree, we remain willing to listen. Listening communicates love.

Love your children through your actions, your tone, and your words. Always. The foundation of love is what holds the framework of good and effective parenting.

APPLICATION

Practice: What is your most natural verbal empathetic response to someone who is experiencing something negative? Examples: "Uh-oh." "Oh no." "This is so sad."

Try responding to every negative behavior your child exhibits with your natural empathetic response.

STORY: HOW THE EMPATHETIC PHRASE UH-OH CHANGED THE LIVES OF ONE FAMILY

Kristy and Brock were so tired of nagging their girls. The seven-year-old twins were very creative and loved to work on art projects and do puzzles. However, when it was time to clear off the table for dinner or tidy up the room before bedtime, the girls procrastinated, ignored their parents, and whined.

Kristy and Brock used to nag and threaten the girls, often resorting to yelling and sending them to their rooms, then cleaning up the mess themselves. This resulted in a negative environment where even Kristy and Brock found themselves being short-tempered with each other.

However, when Kristy and Brock began combining natural consequences, such as making the toys disappear for a while when the parents cleaned up, with an empathetic response like *uh-oh*, an amazing thing happened. After telling the girls that it was time to clean up and then being ignored, Kristy and Brock discovered that all they had to do was sweetly say *uh-oh* and the girls scrambled to clean up. The girls had quickly learned that when their parents expressed sadness, it meant something was not going to go well for them.

"The Uh-Oh Song" is further elaborated on in Cline and Fay's book *Parenting with Love and Logic*. (Note 14.)

Practice: The next time you find yourself getting very angry or frustrated with your child, take three deep breaths while envisioning that you are inhaling love and exhaling anger. If you need more time to process and feel your emotions, communicate to your child that you are currently too angry/frustrated in the moment and that you will address the matter with them later.

KEY POINTS

> ➤ Love is the foundation of all parenting.
> ➤ Pausing prior to responding gives us time to accept our own emotions and consider how our delivery might be perceived by our child, and it gives our child time to consider their own behavior.
> ➤ An immediate consequence is seldom necessary.
> ➤ Remaining calm removes the temptation for our child to focus their energy on us.
> ➤ Aim to respond to all negative behaviors with an empathetic phrase, word, or sound.

CHAPTER 5

Part 1 Summary

L et, Lift, and Listen. These concepts tap into fundamental truths that humans intuitively understand about fostering relationships with others. They serve as the basic building blocks for human connections and personal growth. Let, Lift, and Listen resonates with parents who desire to be the best parents they can be for their deeply loved children.

Punishments disconnected from children's behavior and accompanied by parental anger strain relationships and diminish our influence. We let logical consequences teach our children because we are kind, loving, and compassionate, and because we yearn for our children to make choices that foster their personal growth and help them become the best versions of themselves.

We lift our children with honest and sincere appreciation for who they are. We recognize that all humans long for others to notice what is good, true, and right about us, even when we are not at our best. Because we know our children better than anyone else, our opinion of them matters the most. When they don't believe in themselves is when they need us to believe in them most.

We listen attentively to our children because we understand how important it is for all humans to be valued for their thoughts and ideas. We acknowledge that some of our own ideas and rules may sound as absurd to them as theirs do to us. Therefore, we extend the same respect we expect by listening with a sincere desire to understand and learn from them—their ideas, their thoughts, their emotions. We refrain from irritating our children and attempting to control conversations by bombarding them with questions. Instead, we employ door openers. Our sincere desire to listen to and learn from our children is an act of love and respect.

I have witnessed countless families apply these fundamental principles, and it has been my joy to observe the growth in their relationships, the increase in their own and their children's confidence, and the newfound enjoyment of life beyond their expectations. Like the parents sitting in my office, Suzanne and Cliff, Isaac and Elisha, and Zach and Ashley, they have discovered that by using these principles with the people they most care about, they are communicating deep love and devotion.

As I have learned to apply the principles of Let, Lift, and Listen within my own home, I have discovered that it is never too late to improve and nurture relationships. Although there are no guarantees that our children will become perfect adults, we can lay a solid foundation from which they are most likely to develop their own unique way of thriving in this world. May you and your family find a joy and love that exceeds your wildest dreams.

PART 2
USING THE LET, LIFT, AND LISTEN FRAMEWORK IN THE REAL WORLD

The following stories illustrate how parents apply the Let, Lift, and Listen framework to their unique situations. So often I hear parents exclaim, "You must be living in my house," as the stories I share are representative of what goes on in the lives of all families. All of these stories are based on real families and situations, although some have been modified to protect confidentiality and, at times, to more succinctly illustrate the concepts.

According to the US Census Bureau, in 2022, the majority (70.1 percent) of children live in two-parent families while 25.8 percent of children live with a single parent; the remaining belong to diverse family structures. (Note 15.) Although these stories represent various situations, the concepts and framework remain consistent and true across all family structures.

The foundation of Let, Lift, and Listen applied in an atmosphere of love and empathy makes life better for all. Join me now and imagine how you might apply Let, Lift, and Listen to your own life and family.

CHAPTER 6

Preschoolers

CLAIRE STEALS A COOKIE

Four-year-old Claire asked her mom for a cookie. Mom responded kindly, explaining that it was too close to dinner and that she could have one afterward. While Mom was busy in the other room, Claire took matters into her own hands. She dragged a chair to the counter, climbed up, and helped herself to a cookie. When Mom came back into the room, she saw the chair, the open cookie jar, and Claire wiping crumbs off her guilty-looking face.

Mom could have asked Claire if she had eaten a cookie, but she knew that setting up a child to tell a lie would only complicate matters (see the parenting tip on lies in chapter 8). Instead, Mom commented, "Looks like you decided to have a cookie before dinner. This is so sad."

Claire immediately claimed she had *not* had a cookie. Mom, focusing only on the main issue of Claire disobeying her instructions and understanding that young children sometimes believe their words can alter reality, simply stated the truth. She said, "Sweet Claire, what you really mean is that you *wish* you hadn't eaten a cookie because you know Mommy told you not to. This is not going to work out very well for you."

After dinner, Mom brought out the cookies and distributed them to everyone, along with a little scoop of ice cream. When Claire started crying that she wanted one, Mom softly acknowledged how much Claire wanted dessert but reminded her that she had chosen to have hers before dinner. Mom was well practiced at offering empathy as she let the consequences do the teaching.

Claire, however, was not happy. She started crying and yelling.

Dad, who was also adept at Let, Lift, and Listen, calmly remarked that the screaming was hurting his ears. He asked Claire if she would like to stay at the table quietly, play quietly in the toy room, or go to her room to express herself. Claire continued crying, so Dad asked if she preferred walking or being carried to her room. She was still crying as Dad gently but firmly carried her under his arm to her room. Shutting the door, he said, "We'll miss you, but feel free to come out as soon as you're calm."

The crying persisted for a few minutes while the rest of the family enjoyed their dessert. Eventually, Claire came out, and Daddy welcomed her back with a hug. He asked if she would like to play a game with him.

Parenting Tip: Giving Choices

In this story, Dad skillfully provided choices to Claire. No one appreciates being given orders, so offering children a lot of choices respects their need for developing independence. Dad also understood that when Clare continued crying, she was communicating a choice. Her choice was for Dad to kindly but firmly put her under his arm and carry her. He also gave her the option of deciding when to calm down, which would allow her to leave her room. Had Claire come storming back out screaming, she might have then been given the choice of being in her room with the door locked or unlocked.

A driving force in a child is their desire for independence and autonomy. We want our children to eventually live autonomously, just as much as they desire it. It is a shared goal, not a battle. The desire for independence is apparent from the time a baby learns to say no. An environment supporting autonomy fosters commitment, effort, and high-quality performance. (Note 16.)

Consider your child's perspective on a typical school day. They are told when to wake up, what to wear, where to go, what to think about (math, music, or science), when to eat, when to be quiet, and so on. Essentially, our children are being bossed around all day. Their need for autonomy is denied from the moment they wake up in the morning. It's no wonder they explode when they come home and we tell them to sit down and do their homework.

Parents who understand their child's need for, and lack of, autonomy become adept at providing as many choices as possible, from toddlers choosing between the red or the blue shirt, juice or milk, or brushing their teeth standing up or sitting down, to the teenager deciding whether to do homework before or after dinner, take the bus or get a ride, or sleep in or get up early on the weekend.

You can never give too many choices. In fact, if you provide enough choices, a child becomes more receptive to you making some choices as well. It's important to remember a few guidelines for giving choices:

➤ All options must be acceptable to the parent.
➤ A child refusing to make a choice is actually choosing for the parent to make the choice.
➤ Choices should not be veiled threats, such as "Would you like to clean up your room or be grounded for the weekend?" A more appropriate choice would be "Would you like to clean up your room before or after dinner?"

CALEB AND THE DINOSAUR SHOES

Mom was feeling a bit overwhelmed as she prepared for a family vacation. With a three-year-old and an infant, it was difficult to get anything done. She loaded the children into her car and drove to the department store to purchase some needed items. Three-year-old Caleb was particularly excited about the new shoes his mom had promised him. Upon arriving at the store, he pleaded to go right to the shoes. Wisely, his mom decided to pick up a few other items first, assuring him that his patience would be rewarded. Eventually, they made their way to the shoe department, where Caleb was overjoyed with the dinosaur sandals they found. With only a few more items on her list, Mom made the mistake of pushing the cart past the toy department.

Caleb spotted a large toy dinosaur. He absolutely had to have this amazing creature. He pointed to it excitedly. When his Mom declined his request, he threw a tantrum, screaming and yelling that he *needed* that dinosaur. Mom calmly explained that if he continued, they would have to leave the store without buying anything. Caleb only screamed more loudly and even resorted to spitting at his mom. Mom tried valiantly to ignore her embarrassment and the stares from other shoppers. Little did she know that instead of judging her, they had compassion for her. They were just grateful it wasn't their child this time. Mom moved toward the store entrance, silently praying Caleb would calm down.

He did not.

Upon reaching the exit, she apologetically nodded to the store clerk as she unloaded her baby and three-year-old Caleb, leaving behind the needed contents of the cart to be put back. By now, Caleb was howling about the dinosaur shoes left behind. Mom firmly but calmly wrestled both kids into their car seats. As Caleb arched his back, she used a gentle but firm hand in that well-known belly push to position him correctly. All the while, she murmured kind and empathetic words. "You're really angry." "You really wanted that toy." "You're sad about those shoes." Even if he could not hear her over his yelling, she was helping herself maintain a mature and compassionate demeanor, naming his emotions and assuring him that the situation was safe and under control.

With both children securely strapped in their car seats, Mom took her time walking around the front of the car to the driver's side. She took this moment to breathe deeply and remind herself that her actions were driven by love. She knew that this brief walk might be the only moment of solitude she would have until the children were tucked in for the evening, so she savored it.

As she drove away, Caleb finally stopped yelling, and Mom could feel his angry gaze burning into the back of her head. She turned on her favorite radio station and started humming along, making it clear to Caleb that she was not upset about what had happened. She knew that this communicated to him that he, and only he, was responsible for the loss of his shoes. Deep inside, Mom was almost crying out of frustration. She still needed the items from the store, yet she knew that giving in would only serve the immediate moment, stealing the opportunity for Caleb to truly understand the consequences of throwing a tantrum in a store.

The next morning, Caleb approached his mom and said, "Get the dinoshoes? I sorry. I be good." She smiled, hugged him, and assured him that they would return to the store that day and perhaps the shoes would still be available. Fortunately, the shoes were still there, and Caleb was a perfectly behaved little boy, even telling his little sister to stop fussing so that Mommy could get the shopping done.

This mom knew that even though this lesson was a lot of trouble for her, using the Let, Lift, and Listen approach would yield benefits for future shopping trips.

Parenting Tip: Stop Reminding

When Mom took Caleb to the store the next day, she was careful not to remind Caleb about what happened the previous day. Clearly he remembered.

If Mom had lectured him, saying, "Remember what happened yesterday? If you throw another tantrum, we'll leave, and you won't get those shoes," what message might Caleb have received?

> ➤ You're not smart enough to learn or remember.
> ➤ I'm the one in control here. (Remember, all children desire control, and Caleb is actually quite in control of whether he gets the shoes or not.)
> ➤ I'm mad at you.

Moreover, communicating these messages through reminders or lecture would have been hurting her relationship with Caleb.

A simple statement like "I sure hope the shoes are still available" made Caleb feel like they were a team. Remember, parents who focus on building relationships rather than on breaking them down usually end up with more influence over their children in the long run. As a general rule, if you have already told your child something, there is no need to repeat it. Let the consequences do the teaching instead.

AMELIA LEARNS ABOUT GRAVITY

Maria cherished her role as Amelia's caregiver and treated the eighteen-month-old as if she were her own. However, mealtime had become a battleground. Amelia had discovered that dropping her food over the edge of her high chair tray resulted in some amusing action! She would squeal with delight as Maria got down on her hands and knees to pick up the apple slices, wash them off, and return the food to the tray, lightly scolding Amelia for her actions. She repeatedly told her to eat her food and stop throwing it, but Amelia merely smiled and continued the delightful game.

Amelia's mother had explained the Let, Lift, and Listen framework to Maria, and she contemplated ways to use this approach to change the dynamics at mealtime.

Later that day they visited the park, where Amelia had a blast dropping acorns off a little slide, climbing down to pick them up, then doing it all again. She loved the game, and Maria "lifted" her by commenting on her climbing ability and creativity.

The next time Amelia dropped her food off the tray, she smiled and remarked, "Look at how that falls. It's just like the acorns. It seems like you're having fun playing, so I guess you're done eating." She swiftly removed the rest of the food and took her out of the high chair. Amelia was surprised and upset because she genuinely wanted to finish her snack.

Maria didn't wait long before giving Amelia another chance. She was amazed by how quickly Amelia caught on. She watched as Amelia held a cracker over the tray's edge and looked at her. Kindly, Maria asked, "Are you done eating, Amelia?" In response, she quickly stuffed the cracker into her little mouth.

CORY THROWS A TANTRUM

Mom and Dad were putting dinner on the table for the family when five-year-old Cory began marching around the room with his musical instruments, growing louder and louder and hitting the furniture with his drumsticks. Despite Dad's request for him to stop, Cory only escalated the volume and hit the furniture harder. In response, Dad took away the drumsticks, prompting Cory to throw himself on the floor and unleash a screaming tantrum. Dad's first inclination was to grab him, scold him, and put him in his room for a time-out. The frequency and severity of these tantrums seemed to be getting worse, causing both parents to struggle with their patience. This time, instead of reacting impulsively, Dad took a deep breath, paused, and remembered to Let, Lift, and Listen.

Dad walked over to Cory, let out a sigh, and expressed, "Oh no. This is so sad. It seems like you're having trouble playing nicely and listening to Daddy. This is no fun for the rest of us. That's not a problem. You can take a few minutes by yourself to settle down." Whether Cory could hear Dad amid his screams was irrelevant; what mattered was that Dad remained composed.

As Cory continued his tantrum with thrashing and screaming, Dad calmly picked him up and carried him to his room, commenting on what a strong little boy he was. Using a gentle voice, Dad reassured him, "It's okay, Cory. You may come out when you've settled down. We'll miss you while you're gone." The tantrum persisted for a few more minutes until Cory eventually quieted down and emerged from his room. Mom and Dad welcomed him without any further comment.

Later that evening, Mom and Dad discussed the incident, attempting to identify its cause. Were Cory's actions a result of boredom, fatigue, hunger, or perhaps an attempt to seek attention in other ways before resorting to the loud parade? This is an example of how his parents were listening to him by observing and considering his behavior. Even though Mom and Dad might make some changes in the future that may reduce the tantrums, it was not wrong of them to impose a consequence in the moment. They understood that in real life, people who behave in a manner that make them not fun to be around often find themselves alone.

JACKSON WON'T CLEAN UP

Courtney sighed as she entered the playroom. The floor wasn't even visible under the piles of books, blocks, cars, trucks, papers, pillows, and blankets. What was that red stuff on the couch? And why were there pieces of yarn hanging from the ceiling fan? She had been in the other room for just a moment and now the playroom looked like a tornado had blown through. All her hard work and organization had been undone in a matter of minutes. How could a five-year-old make such a mess? Just looking at it exhausted her. Jackson darted past her and raced down the hall toward his room, undoubtedly planning to wreak havoc there as well.

She asked Jackson to come back and clean up the playroom with her. He ignored her and continued running toward his room. By the time Courtney caught up with him, he'd managed to drag his hand along his toy shelf, knocking all the toys to the floor. Courtney lost it. "You are such a bad boy, Jackson! Come and clean up your toys. *Now!*" Tears welled up in Jackson's eyes as Courtney grabbed his little arm and half dragged him back to the playroom. He continued to refuse, leading to a standoff. Courtney begged, pleaded, explained, threatened, and even spanked him but eventually gave up. When Dad walked through the door, Jackson was crying in his bedroom, and Courtney was furiously tidying up the playroom.

After putting Jackson to bed that night, his angelic face defying his earlier devilish behavior, Courtney and her husband finished cleaning up the playroom while devising a better approach to handle the situation. This time organizing took a bit longer, as they rearranged and used the top shelves in the office to store some toys.

The following day, Jackson was surprised to find only two of his favorite toys in the playroom, the train set and the fish puzzle he loved so much. There were also four of his preferred books on the shelf. He quickly took out the trains, puzzles, and books, then asked for his car racetrack. "No problem, Jackson. I'll get your cars when these toys are cleaned up."

Jackson pleaded, cried, and whined. Courtney was careful not to lecture or remind him how he refused to clean up his toys. In fact, she found ways to lift him. She commented, "You do love playing with your toys. And look at how you arranged the train set. You're so creative and fun. You may have your cars once these toys are put away."

Jackson tried another tactic. "I hate cleaning up. It's no fun and so hard. I'll never get to play with my cars again." Tears started flowing.

Courtney gave him a warm hug and agreed that cleaning up wasn't as much fun as playing.

"So can I have my cars?" Jackson asked.

Courtney kindly replied, "What did I say?"

Jackson scowled and started throwing his train set back in the box. Courtney commented on his good aim!

Eventually, the trains and puzzle were put away, and he asked for his cars. Courtney asked if he was finished reading the books scattered on the floor. She was careful not to tell him what to do, knowing that no one, especially a five-year-old, wants to be bossed around. He quickly put the books away, and Courtney retrieved his car set, carefully placing the train set back in its place on the high shelf.

Later, Jackson asked to go to the park, and Courtney said she would love to take him after his cars were put away. She did not tell him what to do; she simply stated what *she* was willing to do.

Jackson didn't always put his toys away immediately after playing with them. Yet he quickly discovered that the most effective way to get what he wanted was to take responsibility for tidying up. Courtney made a point of noticing his efforts and the progress he was making in terms of organization and hard work.

Parenting Tip: Enforceable Statements

Enforceable statements tell children what we are going to do instead of telling them what to do. (Note 17.) Enforceable statements are declarations of decisions that are entirely within parents' control.

In the previous example, Courtney doesn't explicitly tell Jackson to clean up before they go to the park. Instead, she states that they'll go to the park once the cars are picked up. This grants Jackson complete decision-making control. Mom is okay if they go to the park or not. Jackson gets to decide.

Enforceable statements are subtle yet powerful. They hold power because they demonstrate respect and honor, and they grant control to the other person. Giving orders or being bossy is disrespectful and disempowering, and it hurts the relationship. The truth is, Courtney cannot force Jackson to clean up. Instructing a *child to do something that a parent cannot enforce may make the parent appear or feel ineffective because the child wins.*

Using enforceable statements can be confusing until you get the hang of it. Here are a few examples:

> *"I listen to children whose voices are as quiet as mine" instead of "Lower your voice" or "Stop yelling!"*
> *"The car is leaving at seven forty-five" instead of "Get in the car by seven forty-five, or I won't drive you."*
> *"I pay for college for children who maintain a B average" instead of "You have to get a B average."*
> *"I serve food to children who are seated at the counter" instead of "Come eat at the counter."*

The way to know if you are making an enforceable statement is to ask yourself if you have the ability to follow through on what was said.

PLEASE DON'T HELP MY KIDS

This Facebook post from 2017 went viral and has been translated into more than ten languages. (Note 18.) I believe its popularity is because it resonates with all parents. Kate Bassford Baker hints at the strength required when feeling judged by other parents, how it feels to say no to your child, and the experience of witnessing your child face frustration as they learn valuable lessons. Thank you, Kate, for writing so eloquently about letting our children learn lessons by not rescuing them.

Dear Other Parents At The Park,

Please do not lift my daughters to the top of the ladder, especially after you've just heard me tell them I wasn't going to do it for them and encourage them to try it themselves.

I am not sitting here, 15 whole feet away from my kids, because I am too lazy to get up. I am sitting here because I didn't bring them to the park so they could learn how to manipulate others into doing the hard work for them. I brought them here so they could learn to do it themselves.

They're not here to be at the top of the ladder; they are here to learn to climb. If they can't do it on their own, they will survive the disappointment. What's more, they will have a goal and the incentive to work to achieve it.

In the meantime, they can use the stairs. I want them to tire of their own limitations and decide to push past them and put in the effort to make that happen without any help from me.

It is not my job—and it is certainly not yours—to prevent my children from feeling frustration, fear, or discomfort. If I do, I have robbed them of the opportunity to learn that those things are not the end of the world, and can be overcome or used to their advantage.

If they get stuck, it is not my job to save them immediately. If I do, I have robbed them of the opportunity to learn to calm themselves, assess their situation, and try to problem solve their own way out of it.

It is not my job to keep them from falling. If I do, I have robbed them of the opportunity to learn that falling is possible but worth the risk, and that they can, in fact, get up again.

I don't want my daughters to learn that they can't overcome obstacles without help. I don't want them to learn that they can reach great heights without effort. I don't want them to learn that they are entitled to the reward without having to push through whatever it is that's holding them back and *earn* it.

Because—and this might come as a surprise to you—none of those things are true. And if I let them think for one moment that they are, I have failed them as a mother.

I want my girls to know the exhilaration of overcoming fear and doubt and achieving a hard-won success.

I want them to believe in their own abilities and be confident and determined in their actions.

I want them to accept their limitations until they can figure out a way past them on their own significant power.

I want them to feel capable of making their own decisions, developing their own skills, taking their own risks, and coping with their own feelings.

I want them to climb that ladder without any help, however well-intentioned, from you.

Because they can. I know it. And if I give them a little space, they will soon know it, too.

So, I'll thank you to stand back and let me do my job, here, which consists mostly of resisting the very same impulses you are indulging, and biting my tongue when I want to yell, "BE CAREFUL," and choosing, deliberately, painfully, repeatedly, to stand back instead of rush forward.

Because, as they grow up, the ladders will only get taller, and scarier, and much more difficult to climb. And I don't know about you, but I'd rather help them learn the skills they'll need to navigate them now, while a misstep means a bumped head or scraped knee that can be healed with a kiss, while the most difficult of hills can be conquered by chanting, "I think I can, I think I can," and while those 15 whole feet between us still feels, to them, like I'm much too far away.

CHAPTER 7

Elementary School Children

LIAM WON'T GET UP IN THE MORNING

Mornings were awful. Eight-year-old Liam refused to get ready for school. He threw tantrums. He stayed in bed. He cried. He yelled. His parents tried everything: pleading, bribing, yelling, and even punishing him. It only got worse. Liam seemed to have complete control over the mornings, and everyone hated it.

One particular morning was especially bad. Dad, already late for work, stormed out of the house, leaving Mom in tears. She was upset with Liam for being impossible and with her husband for losing his temper. And she felt like she was failing as a mother.

After a long conversation with a wise friend who was skilled at the art of Let, Lift, and Listen, Mom and Dad decided to change their tactics. They realized they couldn't change Liam's behavior, but they could change their own. That evening, they sat down with Liam and offered their apologies. Yes, *they apologized to him*. They said they were sorry for getting so angry, for constantly nagging and yelling at him. They promised to stop.

Liam was puzzled. He had been expecting a punishment or at least a lecture for his behavior that morning. Instead, they asked him why he had trouble getting up in the morning. They listened intently as he explained how he just hated getting out of his cozy bed, especially when it was so dark outside. They agreed, even noting how much harder it was now that the time had changed and the mornings were darker. Liam told them they were always yelling at him in the morning. They again apologized for their behavior and told him they were going to stop. Liam also mentioned how much he hated it when he missed breakfast and the extra playtime with his friends at school when he was late. Dad agreed that hanging out with friends was fun, and he lifted Liam by commenting how he had already made so many new friends at school. Dad assured Liam that he understood the fun of hanging out with friends and empathized with Liam's struggle to wake up early.

By now, Liam was really perplexed. His parents weren't angry, and they seemed to understand why he was so upset in the morning and why he wouldn't get out of bed. They had truly listened to him. Then they asked him to make some decisions about what would work best for him. Because they weren't going to nag or yell at him anymore, how did he want to wake up in the morning? Did he want his own alarm clock, or did he want Mom or Dad to wake him up? He said he liked having Dad wake him up. Dad agreed and asked him what he should do if Liam fell back asleep. Liam told him to just wake him up again. Dad responded that this idea would not work for him, as he, too, was trying to get ready for work and enjoyed eating breakfast and reading the newspaper. Liam came up with a plan: Dad could wake him up before he took a shower and then wake him up one more time after his shower. Dad thought this was a fantastic idea. Mom added that she would be ready to take Liam to school at six forty-five so that he could have breakfast and extra time with his friends.

The next morning went smoothly, except for one glitch. Liam failed to get up on time! It took incredible willpower for Mom and Dad to resist the urge to wake him up again. Instead, they sat and tried to enjoy their coffee. Finally, at six forty, Mom walked by Liam's door and casually mentioned she would be ready to go in five minutes. This prompted some scrambling in Liam's room and then he yelled out that he wasn't ready. Mom calmly reassured him that it was no problem and that she would take him when he was ready. At six fifty, he emerged looking quite disheveled. Mom smiled and headed toward the door. Liam started to lag behind and complain about not knowing where his backpack was. Unfazed, Mom calmly mentioned that she would make her bed and would be ready to go when he was. Three minutes later, he appeared at her door with his backpack on, telling her she had to hurry. She smiled to herself, realizing that now he was the one nagging her!

Liam was angry during the ride to school, claiming that Dad hadn't woken him up, and now he wouldn't have time for breakfast and to play with his friends. Mom kindly offered him a granola bar she had tucked into her purse. He said he hated granola bars. Mom remained silent. When they pulled up to school, Liam grabbed the granola bar and jumped out of the car. Mom smiled as she drove away, realizing it had been the calmest morning in months.

Mornings were not perfect. Liam might never be a morning person, but at least their home was calm, Mom and Dad enjoyed their coffee together, and Liam felt better about himself. Liam was so lucky his parents were willing to let him miss breakfast when he was eight so that he might have the skills and self-discipline to get himself up and out the door when he was older and the cost of oversleeping would be much higher.

THE SHATTERED CHRISTMAS ORNAMENT

It was the day after Thanksgiving, and everyone was excited about decorating for Christmas. That morning, Mom and Dad had bundled up young Ethan and James and gone to choose the Christmas tree. Dad set it up in the living room, and Mom retrieved the decorations. The boys couldn't contain their joy and enthusiasm, leaping around the room in anticipation.

As Mom unpacked the Christmas boxes, the boys eagerly grabbed ornaments and started hanging them on the tree. As this turned into a competition about who could hang the most ornaments, Mom chuckled but asked them to please slow down and be more careful.

Opening another box, she smiled as she came across a beautiful glass ornament that her husband had given her on their first Christmas together, back when decorating the tree was a quiet and romantic affair. She carefully unwrapped it, but before she could fully admire it, Ethan reached out for it. James, eager to be the one to hang it up, pushed Ethan aside, causing him to trip and accidently collide with Mom. She gasped as the treasure was knocked from her grasp and shattered on the floor. Tears welled up in her eyes.

Chaos erupted as Dad yelled at the boys. "Look at what you bad boys have done. Your Mom told you to be careful. Go to your rooms. Now."

Defending himself, Ethan shouted back, "It wasn't my fault. James pushed me."

James retaliated by hitting Ethan, who began kicking James. Mom grabbed the two boys, her anger rising as the situation devolved into yet another scuffle that seemed to be occurring more and more frequently. She was losing her temper as things regressed into the fighting that seemed to break out multiple times a day. She screamed, "I have had enough. You boys always ruin everything. Now go to your rooms."

The boys burst into tears as they headed down the hall, still pushing and shoving each other as James whimpered about the candy canes yet to be hung on the tree.

Mom and Dad were still upset, their anger lingering in the air. Dad took charge of cleaning up the mess while Mom sniffled, still overcome with emotion. After about fifteen minutes, Dad approached Mom and tenderly embraced her. They sat together, feeling sad about the ornament and even worse about the way they had yelled at the boys and how the night had been ruined. How they wished they had handled it differently. So they decided to take a few minutes and devise a plan, employing the principles of Let, Lift, and Listen to try to salvage the rest of the evening.

Dad made a cup of tea for Mom, then quietly entered the boys' room. Ethan and James had been working together to build a fort for their stuffed animals. Sitting down on the bed, Dad gazed at his sons, their expectant eyes anticipating another scolding or punishment. To their surprise, they saw a soft and affectionate expression on his face.

"I'm sorry for yelling at you," Dad said sincerely. "You did not deserve that. You're not bad boys, and I regret saying those things."

The boys just looked at him, processing Dad's words and feeling perplexed by his unexpected tenderness.

He continued lifting them by remarking, "Look at how nicely the two of you are playing here. I know you love each other and usually get along so well."

Still uncertain, the boys maintained their silence. They had expected Dad to be angry and were unsure of what to make of their father's change in attitude.

Then Dad said, "Mommy sure was sad about the broken ornament."

Ethan interrupted to say, "It was James's fault. He pushed me. He always tries to go first."

Daddy listened and replied, "Yes, when we get excited, we sometimes want to go first. It can be difficult."

James, feeling slighted, whined, "But Ethan hit me."

Dad sympathetically responded, "Yes, I saw that, too. It must have hurt." He continued, "What about Mommy? Can you think of anything you can do to help her feel better? She's very sad about the ornament."

Ethan's face lit up as he eagerly suggested, "You should buy her a new ornament, Daddy."

Dad smiled warmly. "You're so full of great ideas, Ethan."

Not wanting to be outdone, James chimed in, "Let's get her two!"

When Dad reminded the boys that he had been the one to pay for the ornament that had gotten broken and perhaps he shouldn't have to buy a new one, Ethan immediately grabbed his piggy bank. "How much money will it cost, Daddy? I can pay for it!"

James dashed off to retrieve his own piggy bank, insisting that he help pay for it, too. Daddy agreed that it was a good plan and then asked, "What should we do now? Mommy is very sad."

Ethan suggested that they all go out and give Mom a big hug and say they were sorry, just as Daddy had done to them. James added, "And can we have a candy cane?" Dad tousled his little head affectionately as they went back to join Mommy.

Later that week, Dad encouraged Mom to relax at home while he and the boys did an errand. They embarked on a mission to find a special glass ornament for Mommy, and Daddy graciously let the boys use their own money to make the purchase. Dad even stopped for a treat on the way home. The result was a valuable lesson learned, a memorable outing for Dad and the boys, and a tranquil evening at home for Mom.

Forever after, as the ornaments were hung each year, the tale of the broken ornament would be recounted as a family story. The ornament the boys had purchased with their own money became even more precious than the first one.

Parenting Tip: Guilt-Free Parenting

Every parent, including myself, has behaved in ways toward our children that we come to regret. Sometimes it's in action and other times in words. As you reflect on mistakes, know that you are not alone. Every parent who has ever existed has experienced similar moments. When we find ourselves overwhelmed, angry, tired, scared, or frustrated, we often speak from our emotions rather than from a place of logic. It is important to acknowledge that no good parent intentionally wishes to harm their relationship with their children.

One way to reduce the frequency of actions or words we regret is by harnessing the power of the pause (see the parenting tip on this topic later in the chapter). And yet we will still have our parenting fails. However, these failures can be opportunities for us to model to our children what it means to ask for forgiveness and a chance to start anew—a redo. Going back to a child and explaining, without making excuses, our words or behaviors might look like this:

> "Son, please forgive me for what I said to/yelled at you yesterday. I was very angry, and in my anger I said some things that I deeply regret and am sorry for. You are absolutely not (lazy/stupid/spoiled). In fact, you are (hardworking/smart/generous). Just look at the way you (give an example from their life). Please forgive me for saying you are (lazy/stupid/spoiled). You are not. May I have a redo and say what I wish I had said?"

Afterward, we can address the specific behavior directly. Good parents describe an action as bad without labeling the child as bad. Furthermore, we can modify the consequences in this process. Modifying a consequence with an apology and an explanation differs significantly from not following through. Instead of grounding our child for the rest of their life, we can let them know that, due to their failure to be honest about their whereabouts, they will need to stay close to home for a few weeks.

If we never tell our children we are wrong and then seek forgiveness from them, we may unintentionally convey the message that we always mean what we say or do without error. As for myself, when I have a parenting fail, I want my children to understand that we all make mistakes and can recover from them. In my best moments, I will rephrase my thoughts in a manner that enables them to continue believing the best about themselves, even in the midst of their own mistakes.

Another feeling many parents have in common is regret over how we may have parented our children when they were young. Perhaps, as you have read this book, you find yourself wishing you had done certain things differently. It is never too late. We can always sit down with our older or adult children, ask for forgiveness, and tell them what we genuinely believe about them.

Another source of guilt stems from confusion about others' expectations and comparing our family to others. Photos posted on social media showcase the best moments, and although we are aware of this, our own lives may appear duller and more complicated compared to the curated images we encounter on our computers or phones. This is one of many reasons why it is beneficial to limit our social media usage.

Well-meaning friends and parents often give us advice that can seem like judgment and can sometimes make us feel inept. It's okay for others to have opinions; however, their opinions do not diminish your capacity to make sound decisions for your family. Wasting even a moment of time engaging in arguments and being offended or upset only robs you of the time and energy you could devote to focusing on your child.

Instead, it is beneficial to grant the advice giver the benefit of the doubt and assume that their intentions are well meaning. A constructive response to these suggestions or comments is to thank the person and consider their viewpoint. Remember, though, that you know your own child better than anyone else, and ultimately you get to choose to do what you believe is best.

DAD IS MORE FUN THAN MOM

Seven-year-old Mason and ten-year-old Cayley had spent the weekend with their dad at his condominium. Now, on Sunday night, as their mother, Julie, was putting them to bed, Mason whined, "This place is so boring, and you have so many stupid rules. At Dad's, we can stay up as late as we want."

"And we get to eat pepperoni pizza all the time. And hot dogs, and sometimes he grills steak for us," added Cayley.

"And dessert every night," remarked Mason.

Julie was so frustrated. She blurted out, "Well, someone needs to make sure you're healthy and happy, and I suppose your dad just doesn't care."

Mason quickly jumped to Dad's defense. "He does too care. And he's a lot more fun. He even said he's taking us to Disney World over spring break."

Holding back tears, Julie gave them both a hug, said good night, and shut their door. Since their divorce, it seemed like Paul tried to undermine her every chance he got. Julie had always been more concerned about nutrition than Paul, and they used to argue about food issues. He thought she was too strict while she believed he set a bad example for the children. She was a vegetarian and wanted her children to eat the same way. Knowing the importance of sleep and structure, Julie also believed in a strict bedtime routine.

Paul, on the other hand, favored fun and flexibility. When the kids were with him every other weekend and on holidays, he tried to compensate for what he called Julie's controlling nature. He also missed the children and wanted to make every moment with them a good one. Julie felt the need to balance his approach. She now felt like Paul was the fun dad and she was the mean mom.

Julie immediately went to her computer and started typing a lengthy email to Paul, reminding him of the importance of not undermining her, to feed the children healthier food, and to be more aware of their bedtimes. She didn't even know what to say about the Disney trip. She wanted to take the children to Disney, but someone needed to save money for their summer camps this year, and she knew Paul wasn't going to plan for that.

Julie paused from her frantic, furious typing as tears welled up in her eyes. She realized that the same dynamics they had during their marriage were resurfacing, and she hadn't been successful in changing him back then. What made her believe she could change him now?

He used to respond to her lengthy emails with anger, criticizing her for being controlling, accusing her of worrying too much and insisting that the kids needed more fun in their lives. Now he just ignored her pleas for change.

She also knew that he had been saying mean things about her to the kids. And she felt terrible as she remembered the hurt expressions on her kids' faces tonight when she said that their dad just doesn't care. Julie felt overwhelmed and worn out. Instead of sending the email, she wisely saved it and went to bed, making a commitment to meet with a counselor recommended by her friend. Something needed to change.

Her counselor showed great empathy toward her situation and didn't disagree with her beliefs in good nutrition, sleep, and routine. She also agreed with Julie's realization that she never could and probably never would change Paul. The only thing Julie could do was make changes in herself.

Several weeks later, a similar conversation with the children arose. This time Julie was ready to approach it in a more positive way.

"I like it at Dad's better. We get to go to bed whenever we want," complained Mason.

Kindly, Julie responded, "That sounds like fun. How late did you stay up last night?"

Mason enthusiastically shared, "Until midnight. And we had popcorn at eleven."

"Wow," remarked Julie. "You really love popcorn. And you love being in charge of your bedtime."

Surprised that Mom didn't seem upset or angry and didn't explain, once more, the importance of sleep, Mason muttered, "Yeah, I do like to go to bed when I want." Then he had an idea. "So can I stay up late tonight?"

Julie was ready with her response. "Nice try. You know the rules are different here."

"Yeah. I like the rules better over there," mumbled Mason.

Julie didn't hesitate. "I don't blame you. I love you. Good night."

The following night at dinner, Cayley wrinkled her nose at the meal her mom had prepared. "I wish we could have steak or pizza every night like we do at Dad's."

Julie took a deep breath before responding. "Dad truly does like steak and pizza. And he loves sharing those foods with you two."

Cayley agreed. "Yeah. And sometimes I think he eats a little too much meat. I don't think anyone should totally cut it out of their diet, but I think it's better not to eat it every night. Dad says everything in moderation is fine."

"Well, your dad and I have different perspectives," Julie admitted, "and we both love you and want you to be healthy. I agree with him about moderation. Lucky for you, your dad loves steak, too! Maybe you get a good mix in the end."

Mason interjected, "I'm gonna eat nothing but meat and junk food when I grow up."

Julie smiled. "And when you become an adult, you'll have the freedom to decide what you eat every day. That's one of the great things about being a grown-up. For now, you get to eat what Dad and I buy and prepare."

Despite feeling sad about missing the spring break trip to Disney, Julie managed to express her excitement for the kids. She decided to share her big feelings with her friends or therapist, and refrained from burdening the children with these complicated emotions. She chose not to put a damper on Mason and Cayley's excitement. After all, it wasn't their fault that Julie and Paul were divorced. As time passed, her relationship with her children, and with Paul, improved. Although things were not perfect, Julie found solace in the fact that she had alleviated her children's stress regarding the conflicts and disparities between their parents.

Parenting Tip: Rules for Co-Parenting from a Child's Perspective

Dear Mom and Dad,

It's hard enough being a kid, and it is painful that you are not together. Your decision to split up is not my fault. I am sad for you, but I can't do anything to help you with your adult problems. Please just let me be a child.

Please don't say bad things about each other to me or anyone else. It makes me feel sad and embarrassed. Can you say something nice about each other sometimes? You used to love each other, so did all that you loved go away?

And please don't say mean things about each other's families. They are my family too. Let me choose who I care for and who I do not.

If I forget something important at one home, please don't be angry. It's hard for me to keep track of everything. You have one home, I have two. It's not easy for me.

When my other parent or their partner gives my something nice or takes me somewhere fun, please be happy for me. Why would you want me to feel bad about something that makes me smile?

Please don't ask me questions about each other. It confuses me and makes me feel disloyal.

Don't talk about money or child-support to me or within my hearing. I want to feel like your child, not a possession.

Find a safe place to talk about your big feelings without the words accidently falling on my ears. It is not my job to help you with big people problems.

It doesn't feel safe for me if you become my friend. I need you to be my parent. Don't be afraid to set limits. They actually make me feel safe and secure at a time my world is changing.

Don't make me choose where to live. Can you imagine how painful that would be to me?

Don't argue in front of me. That hurts my heart more than you will ever know.

Don't ask me to keep secrets from each other. It makes me anxious and feels wrong.

Please don't send messages to each other through me – written or spoken. This makes me very nervous. There are so many ways to send messages without using me.

Please don't try to get me to take sides in the divorce or explain why it is not your fault. This makes me feel terrible.

Please be friendly and sit near each other at big events. When you don't it is embarrassing and makes me sad. Let my special moments be about me.

You tell me to forgive others, so please show me what that looks like. I know you won't get back together, but hating each other is not good.

Most of all, know that I love and need both of you. Don't be mad if I am mad at you. My feelings are all mixed up. When I am older, I might be able to understand. Right now, I am just a child.

Love, Your Child

THE BROKEN LAMP

It was pouring rain outside, and Mom was busy preparing for weekend company due to arrive later in the day. She was tempted to let the boys play more video games but she resisted, as they had already exhausted their allotted sixty minutes. While she was glad they weren't pestering her about more games, she was not pleased with their wrestling in the living room. At eight and ten years old, Taylor and Ross were growing bigger, and she worried that something would get broken.

Although Mom suggested some quieter activities, the boys continued wrestling. Mom asked them to stop once again, and for a brief moment, they complied. However, as Mom was upstairs preparing the guest room, the wrestling resumed.

Suddenly, a crash echoed through the house—something big had broken. Mom rushed downstairs, horrified to find the living room lamp shattered on the floor, glass scattered everywhere. Thankfully, she did not see any blood, and the boys appeared uninjured. But there was a big mess to clean up, and the lamp was not a cheap one. Naturally, she was furious.

How could she be loving in this situation? Impossible! Knowing the power of the pause (see the parenting tip on this topic later in the chapter), she refrained from immediate words or action. She knew that addressing the issue didn't require an instant response. No one was going to forget what had just happened, and there would be ample time for consequences. Although she was able to refrain from yelling, she knew if she opened her mouth, words she would later regret might come pouring forth. Instead, she covered her mouth with her hand, shook her head slowly, and retreated upstairs.

The boys were bewildered. Weren't they in trouble? Why hadn't Mom yelled at them like she usually did? They stared at each other. Although Mom's behavior seemed odd, they knew they were in big trouble. They quickly started cleaning up the mess.

A few minutes later, Ross went upstairs to check on Mom. He knocked on her door and cautiously asked if she was okay. She assured him she was fine, stifling a smile at his confused and slightly anxious voice.

After fifteen minutes of deep breathing, Mom regained her composure and headed back downstairs. She wore a solemn expression on her face. Taylor and Ross looked up from their cleaning, awaiting her next move.

Mom said, "Thank you for cleaning up the mess, boys. I see you're making sure there's not a single shard of glass left so that no one gets hurt. I'm glad neither of you were injured."

Taylor immediately started defending himself, claiming it wasn't his fault but Ross's. Ross retaliated, and an argument between them ensued. Mom remained silent as she listened. She understood that she might never know the truth and to get in the middle of whose fault it was would only divert attention from the fact that both boys had disregarded her instructions to stop wrestling. Once the boys finished their defense, Mom said, "I didn't witness what happened. All I know is that you two continued wrestling after I asked you to stop, and the lamp is broken. Now what are you going to do about it?"

Silence followed.

Mom continued, "Well, as you finish cleaning up the glass, I want you to figure out how you'll replace the lamp. Let me know on Sunday, once our company has left. By the way, the lamp costs approximately two hundred and fifty dollars."

On Sunday, as the boys were leaving to hang out with their friends, Mom stated, "You boys can go as soon as I know how you're addressing the broken lamp." They rolled their eyes and headed outside to confer.

Very quickly, since they were in a hurry to be with their friends, they found Mom and informed her that they were each going to pay for half the cost of the broken lamp. Ross had the money from his lawn mowing jobs, but Taylor didn't have enough and suggested that Mom could hire him to do some jobs around the house. Mom thought that this was a great idea.

She was tempted to solidify the lesson by reminding them that if they had listened to her and stopped wrestling in the house, this wouldn't have happened, they wouldn't have to spend their money, and so on. But she knew that repeating herself might only irritate them and convey a message that she didn't think they were smart enough to learn from their mistake.

Instead, she chose to offer compassion and lift them. She said, "Ross, I understand that this is difficult. You're a hard worker, and you were close to saving enough money for that bike you've been wanting."

She then turned to Taylor. "The way you meticulously cleaned up that mess showed me how thorough you can be. How about if I hire you to detail my car? I'll show you how, and I'm confident you'll do an excellent job. And then maybe Grandma and Grandpa will want their cars detailed, too. You'll have the money saved up in no time."

In the end, the lamp was replaced, the boys learned some important lessons, and their relationship continued with love and respect.

> ### Parenting Tip: The Power of the Pause
>
> Making Let, Lift, and Listen the framework of parenting requires time and deliberate intention, especially in the initial stages. The act of pausing allows parents ample time to contemplate logical consequences and how to deliver them. It serves as a reminder to approach each situation with love, to actively listen, to establish logical consequences, and even to find ways to lift their child.
>
> Sometimes, as in the story of the broken lamp, a parent may find themselves too overwhelmed to speak. Compassion and calmness become nearly impossible to maintain when anger, exhaustion, and frustration loom large. It is in these moments when we often say or do things that we deeply regret and when we know we could have acted in a better way. The good news is that raising children is not like training a dog. Dogs require immediate consequences, whereas children do not.
>
> Knowing that opening the mouth might unleash a series of deeply regrettable words, a gasp, a horrified look, and walking out of the room can suffice and create space for a pause. A parent might truthfully say, "I'm too upset to think/talk about this right

now. We'll discuss it later/tomorrow." And for added impact, "Don't worry about it for now."

The relief we discover through pausing can give greater clarity. Sometimes we realize that the situation really does not require any action or words. Other times, we must go back and address the issue when everyone is in a calmer state of mind. Resist the temptation to "forget" the problem if it really does need to be addressed. Never underestimate the power of the pause.

I MUST HAVE A CELL PHONE

Allison had been begging for a cell phone since third grade. Her parents were shocked when they discovered that some children as young as first grade already owned one. Although they recognized that it was inevitable, they were adamant about not allowing her to have one at such a tender age. Thus far, they had used the Let, Lift, and Listen framework to uphold their decision.

Mostly, they had listened attentively and empathized with their daughter. Even when Allison exaggerated, claiming that all the other kids have phones, her parents had acknowledged her feelings, saying, "It's got to be difficult. You really want one, too." When Allison got angry and yelled, "You're so mean," they empathetically responded, "It certainly must feel that way."

Allison had repeatedly asked, "But why?" After explaining their reasons to her a couple of times and knowing she had heard them, they started responding to this question with one of their own: "What did we say?" They had learned that continuing to explain implied room for negotiation, giving her a glimmer of hope and often leading to prolonged arguments.

They had even found ways to lift her by saying things like "You certainly are persistent. That will take you far in life. And in this case, it will not get you a phone." "You have a knack for debating and a genuine interest in technology. Those are valuable skills to have in this day and age."

However, sometimes Allison's persistence became exhausting, and her parents knew they were reaching the limit of their patience. During those moments, they established boundaries and presented choices. For instance, they would say, "I really don't want to talk or hear any more about this. You may either change the subject or take yourself to another room." If Allison refused to stop talking about it or leave the room, Mom and Dad would be the ones to relocate, either to another room, the back porch, or even to a nearby coffee shop.

With Allison preparing to go into sixth grade, Mom and Dad contemplated the idea of getting her some type of phone. They appreciated the benefits of a cell phone or perhaps an electronic watch that would allow communication. They would be able to stay in touch with her as she gained more independence, and they could even track her to ensure her safety. They understood that technology was the prevalent mode of communication and making plans. It was also used by teachers and coaches for sharing information. Eventually, they came to agree with Allison: she did need a phone.

They were also well aware of the dangers associated with a smartphone. Mental health issues are strongly correlated to excessive social media usage. There was also the inattentiveness resulting from phone use, the possibility of addiction issues, and safety concerns related to child predators and explicit content to worry about. They had heard horror stories about the challenges and conflict some of their friends faced when setting boundaries for their children's technology use.

Allison's parents felt confused, concerned, and nervous about the issue of phones.

The fact that they had remained steadfast in their decision throughout elementary school had set them up for being able to make an intentional decision and establish clear guidelines. Allison had learned to respect and abide by her parent's decisions. No matter how much she complained and pleaded, they had not given in. This new challenge was different, and Mom and Dad had laid the groundwork for dealing with it.

The conversation about the phone involved a lot of listening and lifting. Allison's parents asked about her concerns and what she thought their concerns might be. They really listened and were pleasantly surprised by how well she understood their fears, which were also her own. They knew that there was much more power in giving Allison the opportunity to speak the facts instead of making her listen to them. They lifted her by telling her how much they appreciated her wisdom and awareness.

They assured her that they trusted her intention to control her own usage. They also asked about the parameters she believed were necessary to avoid getting into trouble. Not surprisingly, Allison confidently declared that she did not need any rules or restrictions because she was certain it wouldn't be a problem. Mom and Dad appreciated her confidence and determination. However, they knew that the creators of addictive technology did not have Allison's best interests at heart.

In the end, her parents chose a restricted type of phone and established set limits, including specific times when the phone had to be charging in their room. It was clear that her parents owned the phone. If the rules were not followed, it would be returned to their custody. There were times when it did become a struggle, and the phone would be taken away for varying durations. During those periods, there was genuine empathy for the difficulties that this natural consequence brought about.

Parenting Tip: Navigating Technology with Your Children

Technology offers a wide array of benefits, but it also carries clear downsides and negative effects, such as anxiety, teen suicide, attention deficits, reduced physical fitness, addiction, and exposure to pornography. These concerns weigh heavily on parents in today's world. The ever-changing nature of technology means that we are literally building the bridge as we walk on it.

The good news is that the framework of Let, Lift, and Listen enables parents to navigate any issue, including technology, and maintain a positive relationship with their children. Because a strong relationship leads to influence, it is important to stay within the framework regardless of the decisions you make surrounding technology. Many parents have shared with me that taking away their child's cell phone is their go-to punishment because it is the one consequence that really gets their child's attention. However, it is important to differentiate between a punishment and a consequence, remembering that punishment means inflicting pain, whereas a consequence is more about teaching and can include empathy.

Punishment might sound like "Because you didn't complete your homework, I'm taking away your cell phone." On the other hand, a natural consequence might be "I understand how much you rely on your cell phone, and it seems to be interfering with your studies. I will return it to you as soon as you are caught up with your schoolwork. You are welcome to borrow mine when necessary."

Parents should remember that the brightest minds in attention technology and human persuasion are constantly striving to capture their child's attention. Your child's inability to self-regulate their own technology use is not a reflection of them being disobedient as much as it stems from the fact that their brains, and arguably all of our brains, are unable to effectively counter the latest technological advancements. When you or others assume that your child should be able to rely solely on willpower and obedience to control their use, you are overlooking the asymmetry of power between your child's brain and the supercomputers behind platforms like TikTok or any other social media app. These platforms are specifically designed to keep your child coming back.

Likewise, difficulties controlling technology in your home are not a reflection on you as a parent. Some argue that it's the parents' responsibility to monitor, control, and educate their kids about all the technology they encounter. However, with technology evolving at an exponential rate and your children using apps you've never heard of, how can you possibly know the intricacies and feature sets and design of all these different apps? It's not possible.

Finally, I am filled with hope because it seems the tide has turned. Most people, including politicians and leaders in the industry, recognize the dangers of uncontrolled access to persuasive technology, especially for teens and children. Steps are being taken to design and implement regulations that will make it a safer space.

In the meantime, adopting the perspective that the negative effects of technology are the enemy (not your child) and viewing yourself and your child as a team fighting for their health and well-being can help maintain a positive relationship. Acknowledging the external factors at play and working together can foster a sense of unity and understanding in navigating the challenges posed by technology.

CHAPTER 8

Adolescents and Teenagers

WHERE IS MY BEER?

It was a beautiful afternoon, and as Dad did some yard work around his home, he noticed a red cooler cleverly hidden under a bush. He sighed, thinking, *Darn kids leave things all over the place*, as he made his way over to retrieve it. When he lifted the cooler, he noticed its weight and decided to open it. To his surprise, it was filled with beer, although he was not entirely shocked because lately he had been growing suspicious of his sixteen-year-old daughter, Jordan. She had been acting a bit secretive and hanging out with a new crowd of friends who seemed like they may be into the party scene a bit. Dad was fairly certain the beer belonged to her.

Dad was actually quite pleased with this discovery. Now he had the proof he needed to make her behave. With newfound determination, he walked back up the hill, eager to confront Jordan with the evidence. Now he had reason to ground her and make her stop seeing those friends.

Fortunately, she wasn't home, so he was forced to pause. As he and his wife waited for Jordan to return home, they considered how they could approach the situation using the Let, Lift, and Listen framework. Together, they devised a plan. It was such a creative idea that, as they chuckled about it, they realized their anger had started to fade away. Their emotions shifted from anger toward their daughter to genuine concern. They started feeling compassion for the potential consequences she would face.

Dad gave the beer to a friend. They would later drink it together as he recounted the tale that was to become a family story for years to come. He then headed to the store to purchase a selection of wonderful nonalcoholic beverages. He filled the cooler with fruit juice, soft drinks, and flavored sparkling waters. He added a note, telling Jordan he hoped she would enjoy the drinks, which were more appropriate for her and her friends than beer. Carefully, he returned the cooler to its original hiding spot behind the bushes.

The following weekend, Jordan retrieved the cooler and put it in the trunk of her car. She planned to meet her friends at a favorite teen hangout out in the country. One of her friends had promised to bring a couple of bags of ice to chill the beer. After Jordan arrived and her friends gathered around the cooler, they discovered the swap. Initially they were annoyed but soon started laughing, telling Jordan that her dad had really gotten her this time. They shrugged it off, played Frisbee, and enjoyed the nonalcoholic beverages. However, Jordan couldn't fully have fun, as she worried about the upcoming conversation with her dad.

Dad noticed the cooler was gone and really wasn't too surprised that Jordan was avoiding him and keeping a low profile. A few days later, he invited her to join him for lunch at their favorite restaurant. On the way, she burst out with the accusation that he had stolen her beer and that stealing is wrong. She was really mad. Dad listened and empathized with her.

Jordan expressed her embarrassment, and Dad acknowledged that taking the beer had put her in an uncomfortable situation with her friends. He reminded her that if the police had discovered the beer, she may have found herself in an even more uncomfortable situation with some serious consequences. He also emphasized the risk of hurting herself, others, or the car. He listened as she claimed that all the kids drink beer and insisted that it wasn't a big deal. Dad chose not to argue, understanding that engaging in an argument or accusing her of lying would only serve to take the focus off the main issue.

Once Jordan had spoken her mind, Dad reassured her of his love and expressed his concern for her judgment. He acknowledged that even if other kids were drinking beer, it was illegal, unhealthy, and dangerous for her. He and Mom did not approve. Dad explained that as much as they wanted her to have the freedom to drive, they just couldn't sleep well at night worrying that she or someone she was with might drink and drive. To ensure her safety, they would be holding on to her keys for a few months, giving her time to mature a bit more.

They pulled into the restaurant, and Dad treated Jordan to a lovely lunch. She tried to sulk, but deep down she realized that her dad was right and that there was nothing more to be said. Her dad didn't even seem angry, making her own anger feel a little bit foolish.

FIRECRACKERS IN THE MIDDLE OF THE NIGHT

It was a quiet Tuesday night, and all my children were sound asleep in their rooms upstairs. I was awakened from a deep slumber by the popping and crackling of fireworks being lit off our upstairs deck. It was 2:00 a.m. Racing upstairs, I found my fourteen-year-old son, Brian, pretending to be asleep in his bed.

When questioned about the commotion, Brian's eyes popped open, and he explained, "I woke up and had to go to the bathroom. I tripped over the firecrackers on my floor."

Period. End of story. That was his explanation.

Although Brian was not perfect, he knew he would likely get in trouble for lighting off firecrackers in the middle of the night. He knew he would wake up others and that he would probably get caught. The truth was he had all the information he needed. He also had good intentions and the desire to stay out of trouble. I felt a mix of anger and bewilderment. Actually, Brian himself seemed a bit bewildered by his explanation for his actions.

Remembering the power of the pause and the importance of offering empathy, I let out a sigh and gave my nervous son a comforting hug, tucking him in like a young boy. I told him not to worry about it for now. As I left the room, I scooped up the remaining firecrackers—an unwelcome gift from a favorite uncle—and took them with me.

My initial inclination was to be angry at my son for the disruption caused by the late-night incident. I wanted to lecture him about the dangers of firecrackers and the thoughtlessness of waking up our family and neighbors. However, Brian already knew these things, and through much trial and error, I had learned that reiterating what my children already knew only hurt our relationship and implied that they were not intelligent enough to remember what they had been taught.

So, the following morning, I said nothing. Brian appeared a bit perplexed by my forgetfulness. It was more time for him to ponder and consider the consequences of his actions. Several days later, he approached me, asking if he could have the firecrackers back. I simply offered him a sad smile and replied, "I don't think that's a good idea."

He began to argue, and I chose not to engage, remembering that it takes two to argue. He rolled his eyes and stomped out, muttering something about me being mean. It was all right that he was upset, and I understood that it probably did feel unfair to him. I worked hard not to take the bait and yell at him. I knew that if I had, he might have found an outlet for his frustration by directing it toward me. Instead, I let him be angry with himself, hoping that he was thinking, *Next time, I won't light firecrackers in the middle of the night.*

Parenting Tip: The Undeveloped Frontal Lobe

No matter how intelligent or high achieving a child may be, good judgment isn't something in which teens can excel. The rational part of the human brain isn't fully developed until around the age of twenty-five. (Note 19.)

To make things even more interesting, recent research has revealed that while adults tend to think with the prefrontal cortex, the rational part of the brain, children and teenagers process information and make decisions using the amygdala, which is the emotional part of the brain. This explains why a child or teen will often act impulsively based on their emotions. That's why, when your child has made a decision based on overwhelming emotional input, they may struggle to articulate their thoughts regarding a decision that appears illogical. They weren't thinking as much as they were feeling. (Note 20.)

As can be seen in the following illustration, the frontal lobe, which is responsible for impulse control, planning, and other executive functions, is the last area of the brain to fully develop. In fact, it may not reach full development until halfway through the third decade of life. (Note 21.)

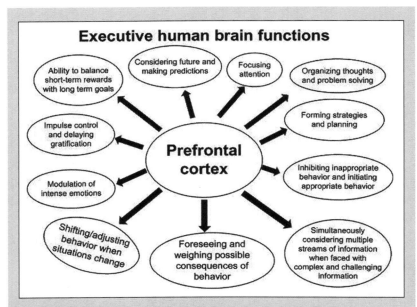

Neuropsychiatric Disease and Treatment 2013:9 449-461
Originally published by and used with permission from Dove Medical Press Ltd.

An undeveloped frontal lobe is not an excuse for poor decision-making and should not preclude logical consequences, whether natural or intentional, set up by caring parents. Nevertheless, understanding the facts about the adolescent brain can give parents hope and optimism for the future, reminding them that their child's behavior is not indicative of being inherently bad, forgetful, or unintelligent but rather a consequence of their developing frontal lobe. Parents should strive to safeguard their children while also assisting them in learning valuable lessons from the consequences they face.

I'VE DECIDED TO QUIT SCHOOL

Fifteen-year-old Bryson stormed into the house after school one day, flung his bookbag onto the floor, and headed straight to the kitchen in search of something to eat. As he was slamming the drawers and cupboards, Mom, using a door opener, commented, "You seem a bit upset," then grabbed a bag of microwave popcorn for him. It was at that moment Bryson declared that he was going to quit school and never return. Sensing this was a time to listen rather than to argue, Mom attentively focused on what he had to say. Bryson began venting about how pointless and irrelevant his schoolwork felt, insisting he would never use any of the things he was learning. Throughout his rant, Mom continued to listen intently. When there was a pause in his tirade, she agreed that she, too, had learned things in high school that she never ended up using.

Bryson was a bit surprised that his mom was not arguing with him about dropping out of high school. Instead, she seemed to understand him and even agree with some things he had said. He continued expressing his frustrations about the mean teachers and unbelievable amount of stupid homework they gave him. Mom responded with soft, sympathetic sounds, letting him know she felt sorry for him and was truly hearing him.

Seizing an opportunity to lift him, she said, "Well, you were placed in those advanced classes because they recognized that you have such a great mind. It does seem you have a lot of homework." Bryson agreed and reiterated his intention to quit school. She knew he needed a safe space to vent his emotions (and get some food in his stomach). Rather than arguing, she made comments that allowed him to reflect on his "decision" to quit school.

Curiously, she wondered aloud, "What would you do if you drop out of school?"

Bryson confidently declared that he would develop a revolutionary video game and make a fortune. Mom continued to lift him, acknowledging his aptitude and creativity, affirming that he was indeed capable of such an endeavor. She asked him about his idea for a game, and Bryson eagerly began describing it.

Taking the conversation further, she inquired how he would go about bringing such a game to the market. Bryson admitted he didn't know. Undeterred, Mom expressed her belief that he could figure it out. As he munched his popcorn, he recounted a story his computer teacher had shared about a friend who had made it big in the game industry. Bryson said, as if to himself, "Hmm, maybe I'll ask that teacher about her friend."

Later that evening, Mom noticed Bryson diligently doing his homework. She refrained from teasing him about this when he had just said he was going to quit school. She felt proud of herself for being willing to listen instead of argue.

Parenting Tip: When Kids Say Something Ridiculous or Alarming

Teenagers often say things that cause parents to fear for their future. They come up with alarming ideas, causing you to forget to listen without jumping in to correct them or to share your wisdom. Staying in the framework, as you continue lifting and listening, will strengthen your relationship with your children, give you information, and allow you to have greater influence on them. Remember, listening does not imply agreement with or endorsement of their unrealistic ideas. You can circle back later and establish some boundaries if necessary.

For instance, imagine your child says, "I have so much homework, I just want to kill myself." Good listening could involve the following conversation:

Mom: "Wow. You sound really frustrated and unhappy."

Teen: "Yes, I hate school and I hate homework. I just can't stand it. It's such a waste of time, and I have so much to do."

Mom: "I see. Is there any way I can help?"

Teen: "Yeah, you could do my homework for me."

Mom: "Nice try. I had to do my own homework at your age. Someday you'll be done with all the homework, but for now it's no fun."

Teen: "That's for sure."

Mom: "Tell me what you meant when you said you wanted to kill yourself."

Teen: "Mom, of course I wouldn't kill myself over stupid homework. I'm just tired of it all."

Mom: "That's what I thought, but whenever you or anyone else says something like that, I'm going to ask about it. It's a serious matter and not something to joke about."

Teen: "Whatever. I just can't do all this homework."

Mom: "Do you want to know what I might do?"

Teen: "No. I don't have time. I just need to get to work and get it all finished."

Mom: "I get it. Would you like me to fix a smoothie for you?"

In this example, the parent actively listened to their child's frustrations, ensured that the comment about self-harm was not a genuine threat, and continued to provide empathy and support. It is essential to address serious statements, establish that they will not be taken lightly, and maintain an open line of communication. In this scenario, the teen only wanted to be heard and made it clear they weren't looking for advice. The mom respected that and showed care and understanding for her child's current situation by offering to make a smoothie.

Remember that every child and situation is unique, and it's important to adapt your approach accordingly. Building a strong relationship based on trust, open communication, and understanding is key to effectively navigating these conversations and supporting your child's well-being.

EMMA WON'T GET UP

At fifteen years old, Emma should have been able to get herself out of bed in the morning. At least, that is what Mom kept telling Emma. And she told her and told her. Every. Single. Day. It was relentless. Emma just would not get up. Mom begged, yelled, and pulled the covers off; she'd even grab Emma's feet and try to drag her out.

Emma preferred getting a ride to school over taking the bus, and because it was on her way to work, Mom did not mind dropping her off. What Mom did mind was chaos every morning and then tension on the way to school. Mom was angry at Emma for ruining the morning and making her late for work. One day she even got a speeding ticket, which *really* made her angry at Emma. Conversely, Emma resented her mom for constantly nagging, lecturing, and yelling at her. To add to the strained dynamics, Mom had recently confiscated Emma's phone as a punishment for making them both late.

In an effort to address the situation more effectively, Emma's mom decided to give the Let, Lift, and Listen framework a try. Here's what unfolded when she implemented the approach.

She seized a fleeting moment when Emma was in the kitchen enjoying a snack and was in a good mood. She pulled up a chair next to her daughter.

"I'm so sorry I got so angry with you this morning," Mom kindly said. She went on to lift Emma. "You don't deserve to be yelled at. In so many ways you're amazing—you're excelling in your classes, especially in that tough chemistry class; volunteering at church; and being incredibly kind to Grandma, who just moved into the garage apartment."

Emma beamed, relishing the recognition for so many good things. Lately, it seemed like every time Mom or Dad spoke to her, they were correcting her. Mom continued, "I really don't want to yell at you in the morning anymore. I don't like to yell at you, and there's no reason for me to get so angry. I lack the patience to wake you up multiple times without getting upset. I've decided to get you any alarm clock you want, since we all leave our phones downstairs after ten. And I will be leaving at six forty-five in the morning to make it to work on time. If you're in the car, I'll drop you off at school."

Emma felt a bit confused. She kind of liked how the conversation was going, but she just had to ask, "What if I fall back asleep? Will you wake me up so that I'm not late?"

Mom was prepared. "Honestly, Emma, I believe you can get yourself up. I will be leaving at six forty-five tomorrow. Do you want me to take you shopping for a better alarm clock? I'm happy to do so."

The next morning, Mom heard the alarm clock go off and then Emma turn it off. Then she heard nothing. It took all of Mom's strength to sit and drink her coffee without waking Emma up. At six forty-five, Mom left for work. At eight, her phone rang.

"Mom!" Emma yelled. "I can't believe you let me oversleep! You left without me! You're so mean. How am I supposed to get to school?"

Mom just listened. When Emma stopped venting, she responded, "That's a problem. What are you going to do?" Silence. "Do you want to know what I might do?" asked Mom.

Longer silence.

Finally, Emma responded, "What? What would *you* do if *your* mom left you sleeping in bed when she knew you needed to be at school?"

Mom kindly responded, "Well, I might call an Uber. Or I might ask Grandma to take me, although I know you're afraid of her driving. Or I might call that neighbor girl who nannies for the family down the street and who doesn't start until ten. She's always looking for extra ways to earn money. Or I might just stay home all day. I'm sure you'll figure it out. See you when I get home."

When Mom arrived home that afternoon, Emma was waiting, seething with anger. She had, in fact, called the neighbor girl. "She charged me fifteen dollars. She said it was cheaper than Uber. *And* I missed my science quiz and had to make it up at lunchtime."

Mom responded with love and empathy. "Wow. Fifteen dollars does seem a bit high. And you work so hard for every dollar you earn babysitting. Missing lunch, which is your favorite time to hang out with friends, couldn't have been any fun. It sounds like a rough day. And I'll be leaving at six forty-five tomorrow morning."

Emma stomped away.

The following morning, Mom was heading out the door at six forty-five when Emma came pushing past her, hair still wet but ready to go. Very quickly, the mornings got so much calmer. Emma felt better about herself, Mom enjoyed peaceful mornings, and sometimes they even woke up early enough to stop at Emma's favorite coffee shop on the way to school.

I WAS AT SCHOOL, NOT THE BEACH

It was a warm sunny day in late April, and Leslie was working from her home office when her friend stopped by. She informed Leslie that she had just come from the beach and had seen Leslie's son, Logan, surfing with some friends. This would not have been a problem except that sixteen-year-old Logan was supposed to be at school. Leslie's friend assured her that Logan hadn't seen her, and she was absolutely certain it was him.

That afternoon when Logan walked through the door, Leslie greeted him pleasantly and motioned toward the brownies she had made. As he munched on them, she kindly asked him how the surf had been. He stopped midbite, quickly composed himself, and proceeded to tell a lie. "What are you talking about? How would I know? I wasn't at the beach. I was at school."

Mom didn't take the bait. She knew that accusing him of lying might derail the conversation. She wasn't even surprised he lied. After all, didn't she do the same when she was a teenager, making up stories to try to avoid getting into trouble? But this was about skipping school, not just lying.

Leslie responded, "You're probably going to wish you had been at school instead of cutting classes and going surfing. No, you were at the beach. Don't worry about it right now. Your dad and I will talk with you about it later this evening. Would you like another brownie?"

Notice that Leslie didn't set Logan up for a lie. She did not ask, "How was school today?" She knew that would divert the focus from the real issue. She did not argue. Nor did she punish or lecture.

Was this easy? Absolutely not. In fact, Leslie was feeling very angry, but she knew that if she engaged in a discussion, she would likely resort to lecturing. It was better to take a pause.

Later, as she cooled down and reflected on her feelings, she realized that she was experiencing fear and embarrassment. She feared that Logan wouldn't graduate, get into a good college, or secure a good job. After further reflection, she realized that ultimately this would be Logan's problem to face, not hers. After all, she had finished high school, attended college, and had a good job. This was his life, not hers. Acting as if his success at school was her own problem might send the message that she would take responsibility for making sure he graduated. This didn't mean she would simply let it go. It was important for Leslie to do what she could to help him get through high school. There needed to be a consequence that might help him learn to be responsible for attending school.

Her embarrassment stemmed from the fact that her friend, whose son would never cut school, had informed her about Logan's actions. Leslie often worried about what others would think of her parenting. While it might be true that some people would judge her, most parents are far less judgmental than we assume. Other parents are busy fretting about their own children and likely feel more compassion than judgment. Leslie and her husband prioritized their child's growth and development over their reputation as parents. She was determined not to let embarrassment lead to anger.

Another reason for her delayed response was that she genuinely didn't know what to do or what consequence might be logical and effective. Thinking on the spot can be challenging, especially when fear, embarrassment, and anger cloud rational thinking. Leslie knew she needed time to consider the situation and to determine a logical consequence. She also thought it would be good to brainstorm with her husband, Alan, to find the most appropriate and effective consequence.

Now let's return to the story.

A look of surprise mixed with confusion crossed Logan's face. Where was the anger he was expecting? What about the lie he just told? Did she believe him or not? Then a look of concern appeared on his face. What would the consequences be? He wished she would just yell at him, punish him, and get it over with. The waiting was more difficult than an argument. In fact, Logan kind of enjoyed arguing with his mom because it made him feel powerful when she would get upset.

Noting his perplexed expression, Mom quickly turned away, suppressing a smile. Her anger was fading, and she was beginning to feel sorry for Logan. She also felt some relief as she realized that she could parent effectively without getting angry.

Leslie was able to explain the situation to her husband prior to his arrival home, giving Alan time to think about it as well.

So what happened?

Alan arrived home and waited until dinnertime to address the issue of skipping school. Using a door opener, he said, "I heard that you decided to go surfing today instead of attending school," then he paused to listen to Logan's reply.

Logan was ready. "Yeah, school is such a waste of time, and we weren't doing anything important anyway. I'm getting good grades, so it really didn't matter. And I only left for the afternoon. I shouldn't have lied to you, Mom. I'm sorry. I won't do it again."

Dad responded, "Thank you, son. It's mature of you to apologize to your mom. So you really feel like school is a waste of time? Tell me more about that."

Logan proceeded to talk about his classes and how boring they were. Dad listened and even found areas where he could agree. He shared his own experiences of finding certain things boring during his high school years.

Dad then took the opportunity to lift Logan by saying, "You *are* getting good grades, especially in your advanced physics class. You really have a mind for science. Maybe that's why you understand the waves so well; it's one of the things that makes you such a good surfer."

After what turned out to be a pleasant conversation, Alan and Leslie addressed the issue of skipping school. First, they let Logan know that they were going to notify the school that Logan had not been absent due to sickness. There was to be no excused absence. It was only fair that the school know what was going on, since they were responsible for him during school hours.

Unbeknownst to Logan, when his parents notified the school, they had a discussion with the principal and encouraged her to impose any consequences she deemed appropriate. The school *did* have a consequence in place, and Logan was required to attend supervised study hall every day instead of his free lunch hour. This was a consequence Logan didn't like because lunchtime was when he got to hang out with his surfing buddies.

When Logan learned from the school about his consequence, he complained to his parents about the stupid rule. They listened and offered compassion. "Oh. That has to be tough, being in study hall with that teacher you don't like while your friends are enjoying their time together. At least this situation is for only two weeks since you've never skipped school before."

Logan's parents decided that they did not need to impose additional consequences. Their goal was for Logan to choose to stay at school, and they believed that the study hall was enough to make him seriously reconsider further temptations to skip school. They were also aware that Logan had been warned by the principal that if he were to cut school again, there would be a much more serious consequence. He might even have to attend summer school, a time when Logan was most looking forward to surfing with his buddies. In this case, Leslie and Alan were fortunate that the school imposed a consequence so that they could strengthen their relationship with their son by offering empathy.

Parenting Tip: Lies

Based on my experience as both a parent and a professional, I've observed that the primary reason children and teens tell lies is to stay out of trouble. If they weren't misbehaving, they wouldn't need to lie. Although very young children may still be learning that words do not make something true, older children need to learn to change their behavior so that lies are not necessary. It's best for *parents to simply state what they believe to be the truth and to keep their focus on the issue at hand.*

Engaging in arguments over the truth, particularly with teen-agers, can often be futile because parents may not always have tangible proof that the child is lying. Instead, wise parents simply focus on the behavior and avoid getting entangled in the lie.

Because honesty is a quality most parents wish to instill in their children, there are instances when it is appropriate to address and discuss the lie. The key is to differentiate between the behavior and the subsequent attempt to cover it up. For example, if a young child sneaks a cookie and then lies about it, the primary lesson should be about obeying the parent. Perhaps addressing the disobedience by missing dessert that evening is all the child needs. On the other hand, a teen who lies about where they're going might need to stay home for a weekend. As one parent explained to their child, "How will we know where you're really going to be when you lied to us last weekend?"

Modeling honesty is also crucial in parenting. If a child wit-nesses a parent lying about the child's age to save money on an entrance fee, it teaches the child that lying is acceptable when personal gain is involved. Therefore, it's important for parents to lead by example and to demonstrate integrity in their own actions. It is difficult to parent well if your own behavior loudly says, "do as I say, not what I do!"

LATE FOR HOCKEY

Her boys loved hockey, and Mom knew it was good for them. However, she was about done with it. On practice days, her two teen-age boys needed to be at the ice rink by seven, which meant leaving the house by six.

This meant she had to start nagging at five thirty. "Hurry up and finish your dinner so that you can load the car." "What do you mean you can't find your jersey? You should have looked for it earlier." "Get off the phone!"

They typically raced off at 6:10 p.m. The boys sat sullenly in the car as Mom lectured them about being on time while scanning the road for police officers armed with radar guns.

One evening while sitting in the freezing ice rink waiting for practice to end, Mom decided she had finally had enough. She devised a plan to let the consequences do the teaching. And so, the next practice day, she put her plan into action.

At five thirty, Mom calmly announced that she would be in the car, ready to depart for hockey, at six. Two minutes before six, she headed out to the car with a book she had been wanting to read. By six fifteen the boys were scrambling out the front door *yelling at each other* to hurry up. As they loaded their gear in the car, Mom continued to enjoy her book. Once everything was loaded, she drove to the hockey rink at the posted speed limit. The boys raced through the parking lot clinging to the hope that they might slide in before the coach noticed they were late. The consequence for being late was push-ups in full gear.

Despite her previous attempts to help them avoid this consequence, Mom secretly found enjoyment in watching her boys struggle through their push-ups. She discovered that the push-ups really didn't hurt *her* at all! Letting the consequences do the teaching was so much easier. And now she could empathize instead of nag.

During the ride home, the boys complained about the push-ups. They attempted to blame Mom for making them late. She resisted the temptation to remind them that she had been ready to take them on time.

Instead, she listened and empathized and lifted. "That certainly did look challenging. I probably couldn't do a single push-up, let alone with all that heavy gear on. You boys sure are strong."

Never again did she nag her boys about getting to hockey practice on time. In fact, at five forty-five when she began looking for her book, the boys would start nagging each other! Their journeys to the rink became more peaceful, filled with conversations rather than lectures. They all learned to like one another a little more, and the boys learned some responsibility, self-reliance, and self-discipline.

THE DREADED PHONE CALL

Mom and Dad were enjoying a quiet evening at home when sixteen-year-old Dominic left after dinner to go to his friend's house. He assured his parents that he and a few other guys were just going to hang out and play video games. He promised to be home by midnight. However, the phone rang at ten thirty. It was the police. They requested that a parent come down to the police station where Dominic was being held. He and some other teenagers had been arrested at a large party on the other side of town, where alcohol, marijuana, and other illegal substances were being consumed.

Both parents were somewhat surprised. Although they knew that underage drinking and substance abuse were a possibility with a sixteen-year-old, so far Dominic had never been in this kind of trouble, nor had he given any indication that he had experimented with alcohol or other illegal substances. Mom was very upset and realized she would not be able to stay calm and practice Let, Lift, and Listen. They decided that Mom would stay home while Dad went to fetch Dominic. The police station was fifteen minutes away, and Dad used the time scripting in his head what he would do and say. Mostly he decided to say very little. He wanted to be loving yet firm. He wanted to maintain a good relationship with Dominic regardless of the outcome or the consequences. He wanted to allow this experience to help Dominic grow and develop into a wise man. Dad hoped the police would enforce appropriate consequences, allowing Dominic to learn valuable lessons without Dad having to be the bad guy.

Upon arriving at the police station, Dad noticed another father berating and yelling at his son in the parking lot. Witnessing the angry and dejected look on the boy's face inspired Dominic's dad to remain calm and wrap this situation in love and compassion.

When Dominic was brought out from the back of the station, Dad shook his head sorrowfully, telling Dominic that he was sad for him because this was certainly not going to end well. After completing the necessary paperwork, they walked out to the car in silence. Dad said nothing. He wore a glum and concerned expression on his face. He even reached over and gave his son a reassuring squeeze on the shoulder.

The ride home was interesting. Dominic started talking. He hadn't been drinking . . . it wasn't his fault . . . he didn't even want to go to the party but his friends convinced him . . . it was his first time at a drinking party . . . the cops had been mean . . . this was all ridiculous. Dad just continued to drive, listening and occasionally responding with expressions like *ah*, *whew*, and even *that sounds rough*. Dominic was confused because he had expected his dad to be very angry. When they arrived home, Dad informed Dominic that Mom was tired and had gone to bed. Dad, too, was exhausted and assumed Dominic was as well. He assured Dominic that they would discuss the matter in the morning and told him not to worry about it. The expression on Dominic's face was priceless; he certainly couldn't help but worry about it.

Of course, Mom was waiting up in their bedroom to hear how things had gone and to discuss the possible consequences. Dominic's parents knew that by not displaying worry, they were sending a message to Dominic that the problem was *his* to solve, not theirs.

Even though it was Saturday, Mom and Dad decided to wake up early the next morning to rouse Dominic. Knowing that Dominic would be tired, waking him up early was a deliberate part of the consequence. They welcomed him to the table where they had prepared his favorite breakfast. Dominic was perplexed. He had been awake most of the night concocting excuses in his mind. What was up with his parents? Was he not in trouble? Dad simply opened the door to the conversation by stating that the previous night had been a bad one.

Dominic started talking. As the string of excuses, reasons, and even some suspected lies came tumbling out, his parents listened solemnly. They refrained from challenging him because they didn't really know what had transpired. What they *did* know was that Dominic had not been where he said he was going and that there had been illegal substances at the party. That was all they needed to know and all they needed to respond to.

Mom and Dad worked hard to lift Dominic even when they weren't sure if he was telling the truth. When he claimed that he hadn't wanted to go but was pressured by his friends, they remarked on how uncharacteristic it was of him to buckle under peer pressure. They reminded him of his usual self-confidence and strength to do what he knew was right. When he asserted that he hadn't consumed any alcohol, they mentioned that it didn't surprise them because they knew he was smart enough to understand the potential harm to a fifteen-year-old's brain cells that alcohol and drugs could cause. Eventually, Mom asked Dominic what he thought would happen next.

Dominic mentioned that based on what others had told him, they would have to pay a stupid $600 fine. Dad shook his head and commented that at least Dominic had saved up just a bit more than that from his hard work cutting grass the previous summer. Too bad that what he was saving—for a car—was going to be used to pay the fine.

Dad inquired about any potential additional consequences, and Dominic shrugged, helping himself to another piece of bacon. When Dad brought up the upcoming lacrosse state championship, Dominic stopped midbite. A stricken look washed over his face as he explained that his coach had a rule: If caught drinking, players had to sit out three games. Dominic expressed hope that the coach might not find out but quickly followed up with a more downcast remark: "But he always does. He probably knows already." With the state championship only a week away, Dominic just had to play. He was the team captain! He pleaded, "Please, Dad, call Coach and tell him that I wasn't drinking and that it wasn't my fault."

Dad seemed to agree. "Yes, I think calling the coach is a good idea. And if I were you, I would make that call before he hears the news from someone else. You are such a leader. You were chosen as captain because all the guys look up to you. Hmm. You certainly do have a problem here. Perhaps the coach will listen to you. Yes. I think calling him is an excellent idea."

As they finished breakfast, Dominic announced that his buddy was coming to pick him up to play basketball. Mom and Dad exchanged glances. Mom informed Dominic that she and Dad were kind of tired from the previous night, and they simply couldn't muster the energy to worry about whether he would go where he claimed to be going. They explained that they needed him to stay close to home for a while.

Dominic wanted to know how long he would have to stay home, to which his parents simply replied that it would be until they felt confident in his honesty regarding his whereabouts. For the time being, it would be great to have him around the house, as there were some tasks that needed attention. Dad mentioned that he was planning to paint the fence that afternoon, and now Dominic would be there to help.

YOU ARE WELCOME TO REPEAT SEVENTH GRADE

Dad reviewed his twin sons' seventh grade report cards. Collin had a mix of As and Bs while Hunter had two Fs and three Ds. Dad knew that Hunter had the same capability as Collin, but this year he had been refusing to apply himself or do his homework. All Hunter wanted to do was skateboard. Dad had always prided himself on helping his boys get their homework done, but recently Hunter had absolutely refused. No matter how much Dad yelled and punished him, Hunter's grades got worse. Even when Hunter managed to complete his homework, he often forgot to turn it in.

Dad was beside himself. He decided to approach the situation differently, using the Let, Lift, and Listen framework. One day he sat down with Hunter and asked him why his grades had dropped. Hunter proceeded to explain that seventh grade was just too hard. The teachers were mean. The homework was stupid, and it was all such a waste of time. Dad had heard these complaints before and, in the past, had deftly argued every point. He now realized that arguing had only made Hunter angry and more determined to prove his point. This time Dad chose to listen and empathize.

"It does seem like a waste of time. I remember feeling the same way when I was your age. In fact, there are some things I learned in seventh grade that I have never used. And mean teachers? That is awful.

Dealing with mean teachers can be a real pain. And if you find it too hard, maybe it really is," Dad said, empathizing with Hunter.

Dad also lifted Hunter by adding that he knew how smart Hunter was and also how hard he worked. He said, "When you put your mind to something, you persevere until you get it. Just look at the way you never stopped trying to learn the kickflip and the ollie on your skateboard. Perhaps seventh grade really is too hard. The good news is that although it's a law for you go to school, there is no rule against repeating seventh grade. Your mom and I will love you just as much, even if it takes you two years to get through seventh grade. It really isn't a problem for us."

Dad went on to mention the potential benefits of being in a different grade from his twin brother, suggesting that Hunter could make friends with the nice kids in sixth grade next year. He handed Hunter his skateboard and encouraged him to have fun. He reminded Hunter that he was there to help him with his homework if he needed it.

Although parents tell me the Let, Lift, and Listen method works like magic, the effect is not always immediate. Did Hunter suddenly start doing his homework and bring his grades up? He did not. In fact, for the next two weeks, he didn't even glance at his homework. Dad stopped reminding him, and Hunter spent all his time skateboarding. Dad was determined to stay the course, but it was difficult.

It was time for further action. Dad set up a clandestine meeting with Mr. Ryan, the assistant principal of the school, and explained his approach. Fortunately, Mr. Ryan was enthusiastic about helping parents who let their children learn from their own mistakes, and he readily supported the plan.

The following day, Mr. Ryan summoned Hunter to his office. Hunter, thinking he was in trouble, sat sullenly in the chair. Mr. Ryan, adept in the Let, Lift, and Listen framework, treated Hunter very kindly. He informed Hunter that they were working on the classroom assignments for the coming year and wanted to know if Hunter thought he would pass his classes and progress to eighth grade. Hunter declared that it was just too hard and that no one, including his parents, was willing to help him. Mr. Ryan listened compassionately and assured Hunter that repeating seventh grade wouldn't be a problem. However, if Hunter simply needed extra help, Mr. Ryan would be more than willing to arrange it.

Shortly thereafter, Hunter got busy doing his homework. He did manage to pass seventh grade, though he just squeaked by.

Hunter's parents understood that the lessons learned in seventh grade would benefit him in the future. They did not want him to be held back a year, yet they knew that learning these lessons at a younger age was generally less costly than learning them as adults. They were willing to let him repeat seventh grade if that was what it took.

At the time of writing of this book, Hunter was in his second year of medical school. He skateboards from class to class.

Parenting Tip: Creating a Family Mission Statement

A family mission statement identifies and articulates your family's core values and helps guide your decisions toward what truly matters. It can enable you and your family to identify your purpose and reason for being, acting as a road map and helping you navigate toward your desired destination. We wouldn't start driving without a destination or embark on a journey without a port in mind. Why would we raise a family without thinking ahead to our purpose?

A well-defined mission statement helps you communicate and teach core values to your children. For instance, if your desire is for your child to excel in science and earn an A, it's important to understand and communicate your underlying reasons behind wanting your child to earn a high grade. Chances are, you probably didn't hope, when your child was born, that she would get an A in eighth grade science class! It is more likely because you value hard work, learning, discipline, or perseverance. Perhaps it's because you want to the keep doors open for her future. If you have not articulated these values, you might mistakenly convey that obtaining an A is the end goal. If that were true, wouldn't it be better for your child to take the easiest class? Most parents would agree that they prefer their child to be interested and challenged and to develop core values such as discipline and perseverance than to take easy classes just so they can earn good grades.

A mission statement clearly reflects your family's values and goals. It not only increases the likelihood of achieving these goals but also strengthens your relationship with your children. For example, if your child lies about their whereabouts and you respond, "It makes me so mad when you lie to me," you are turning the issue into a conflict between your child and yourself. However, if you say, "Honesty is one of our core family values," you shift the focus away from yourself. Instead, you communicate and act as if you are part of the same team, working together to uphold the family's core value of honesty.

Of course, consequences may be necessary for dishonesty. However, by keeping the focus on the mission rather than taking it as a personal offense, you preserve your relationship while communicating a greater goal.

I strongly recommend dedicating time to articulate a family mission statement. There are a multitude of online articles that provide guidance on the topic. Ultimately, each family finds its own unique approach. Here are a few general pointers that work well for many families:

> ➤ *Involve the entire family. This can happen through a formal family meeting or a casual conversation during a meal or car ride. It can occur when you first start forming a statement or after parents have already written a rough draft. If a child chooses not to participate, the assumption will be that they agree with what you have written.*
>
> ➤ *Begin with a list of the character traits and values that are important to all of you.*
>
> ➤ *Write in the present tense, using phrases such as "Our family is . . ." instead of "Our family will be/strives to . . ."*
>
> ➤ *Focus on values rather than on specific actions. Stating that your family will eat dinner together is an action or a plan. If your family mission includes connection, then scheduling regular family dinners becomes an action that supports your mission.*

Your mission statement will be unique to your family. It represents the destination your family aims for and the principles that will guide you along the way. If you veer off course from time to time, that's normal. When that happens, regroup, remind yourselves of your core values, and get back on track.

"A family mission statement is a combined, unified expression from all family members of what your family is all about—what it is you really want to do and be—and the principles you choose to govern your family life." —Stephen Covey said

BENJAMIN PUNCHES A HOLE IN THE WALL

Fourteen-year-old Benjamin was furious. All his friends were going to a party on the other side of town, but his mom, Susan, had forbade him from attending. She was worried about his new group of friends and didn't know the family hosting the party, so she decided that it was not a good idea for him to attend.

Benjamin had always struggled with a volatile temper, and his mom and stepdad had been working with him to control it. It had been six months since his last outburst. However, this situation pushed him over the edge. He yelled at his mom, who calmly instructed him to go to his room and cool off. Fuming, he stomped up the stairs and, upon reaching the top, unleashed his anger by slamming his fist into the wall.

Susan heard a crunch and hoped he hadn't broken his hand. She exercised great self-control, staying silent and waiting. After a moment, she heard his bedroom door slam shut.

Whew. She crept up the stairs and saw a fist-size hole in the wall. She was angry and nervous at the same time. Angry at Benjamin and nervous about how her husband, Ned, would react when he returned home later that day. Ned had just finished painting the upstairs hall, and the hole would undoubtedly infuriate him. Susan was glad Ned wasn't home at the moment.

Susan had married Ned only four years ago, after she and Benjamin's dad had divorced. Benjamin's father now lived on the other side of the country and saw Benjamin only a couple of times a year. Ned had been a supportive stepfather, wisely leaving most of the discipline and final decisions about Benjamin to Susan.

Susan and Ned knew the stepparent relationship would be different from a father-son relationship. They aimed for Ned to have an influential yet uncle-like role in Benjamin's life while Susan maintained her parental authority. They agreed on the Let, Lift, and Listen framework, although sometimes they disagreed on the appropriate consequences. In Benjamin's presence, Ned always deferred to Susan's judgment.

Privately, they might discuss different approaches but kept these conversations confidential. Ned often believed Susan should be more lenient and might even place some blame on Susan for Benjamin's outburst.

Susan made herself a cup of tea and called a friend who also understood the Let, Lift, and Listen framework. They had made an agreement to seek each other's advice in such situations, knowing that an emotionally uninvolved perspective could offer clarity. Her friend listened and helped her plan her next move.

Susan finished her cup of tea, took a deep breath, filled a ziplock bag full of ice, and headed upstairs. Respecting Benjamin's privacy, she lightly knocked on his door. Benjamin responded in a surly voice, "What?"

Mom asked gently if she could come in. She handed Benjamin the bag of ice, acknowledging that his hand must hurt. She remarked, "Wow, Benjamin, I knew you were strong, but a hole in the wall?" She actually lifted him in this moment!

Benjamin looked at her, somewhat confused. "Aren't you angry, Mom? Aren't you going to yell at me?"

Mom just shook her head sorrowfully, commenting that Ned was not going to be happy, and she didn't think that yelling at Benjamin would make any difference. It certainly wouldn't fix the wall, which was now Benjamin's responsibility.

Benjamin shrugged and looked at his bruised and swollen hand. "Well, it doesn't even matter if I break my hand, since I never get to go anywhere anyway."

Susan ignored the comment, left the room, and went outside to text her husband, asking him to call her when he had a moment. When they spoke, she recounted the incident to him. As she expected, Ned was furious. Fortunately, he wasn't coming home until later that day. The delay gave him time to cool off. He told her he would call her back. When he did, they discussed a plan of action.

Upon arriving home, Ned headed to the backyard where Benjamin was shooting hoops. He took the ball and shot a few baskets with his stepson. Using a door opener, he said, "I heard you had a rough day, Benjamin." Benjamin scowled and began venting about how mean and overprotective his mom was. Ned simply listened, neither agreeing or disagreeing. He knew that listening did not mean he agreed. Ned just listened.

Finally, Benjamin asked Ned if Mom had told him about the hole in the wall. Ned said she had. "Aren't you even mad at me, Ned?"

Ned explained that when Mom initially told him, he was indeed very angry. However, instead of rushing home, he decided to think about it. He realized that being angry wouldn't fix the wall.

Benjamin looked relieved. He then told Ned that his Mom had said he would need to pay to repair the hole in the wall. "How much do you think it is going to cost?"

Ned told Benjamin that he knew someone who could repair it and estimated that it would cost around $500, including painting.

Benjamin gasped, alarmed by the hefty price tag. Ned continued, explaining that he knew how to fix it and would be happy to teach Benjamin. The cost of supplies would be much less.

The next morning, Ned and Benjamin headed to the building supply store to gather the necessary materials. By late afternoon, the hole was repaired, and Benjamin had acquired a valuable skill. He was unhappy about having to spend his own money on supplies, but he was relieved that it didn't cost him $500.

At dinner that evening, Benjamin commented that fixing drywall was easier than he thought. If someone would have charged $500 to fix the hole, maybe he could consider getting a summer job with a local builder. Ned happened to know a skilled builder who could mentor Benjamin and offered to help him secure a summer job if he was interested.

CHAPTER 9

Adult Children

The role of a parent never truly ends, regardless of whether our children have recently moved out or have been away for years. As parents, we can continue to have a positive influence and pass on our parental wisdom using the Let, Lift, and Listen framework.

LEAVING A NIGHTTIME MESS

Lucy's son and daughter were coming home from college for the summer. As a single mom, Lucy had missed the kids, but there were aspects of being an empty nester she really enjoyed. One of her favorite moments of the day was waking up to the house the same way she had left it the night before. She could make a cup of coffee and prepare for her day in the peace, quiet, and calmness of an organized and tidy house.

When her children were home, it was a different story. The kids would stay up late, watching movies, making popcorn, and having fun. Even though they had heard their mother lecture and complain and nag, this was not of strong enough consequence to convince them to clean up before they went to bed. And the use of threats and nagging was damaging to her relationship with her almost grown children.

Lucy wanted this summer to be different. She gave some thought to it and devised another approach, considering the idea of letting the consequences do the teaching.

Her daughter, Ava, arrived home first. Mom warmly welcomed her. She was truly glad to have Ava home again. She had missed her children. Before Mom went to bed that night, she did *not* remind Ava to clean up. Instead, she casually mentioned she was tired of nagging and yelling. "I love you too much to badger you, and I don't want to start our summer off by being such a nag." Ava was happy about this.

Instead, Mom explained how she had received a professional massage as a gift and really loved it. They were expensive, though, and she was looking for ways to earn money to have another one. She told Ava that she was willing to clean up the kids' stuff every morning, but she expected to be paid for it. She would charge the going rate for a cleaning person and bill in fifteen-minute increments. Mom would keep a record and divide the cost equally between Ava and her brother, since there was no way to know whose mess it was. When Mom earned the needed amount, she would simply deduct it from the kids' savings accounts, which she held jointly with them, and thank them for the opportunity to earn a massage. No problem!

The next morning, Mom awoke to find a clean house. Then Bryson arrived home from college. Before Lucy had a chance to tell him the plan, she was overjoyed to hear Ava explain Mom's ridiculous idea to Bryson. Later that evening, as Mom lay in bed, she overheard the kids arguing about who was going to clean up the mess in the kitchen. Lucy rolled over and slept soundly, knowing she would wake up to a tidy home.

Mom never earned enough to get a massage that summer. They all laughed together as she started asking the kids to please leave a mess so that she could earn some of their money. They refused.

HOOTING AND SNORTING FROM THE BATHROOM

The noises emanating from the bathroom were disturbing. The combination of running water, hooting, and snorting brought Dan and Judy running. What had Jimmy done now?

At twenty-six years old, Jimmy, their nonverbal son with special needs, seemed to be causing more trouble as time went by. As Dan and Judy rushed to the bathroom, they saw Jimmy in the midst of flushing the toilet repeatedly, causing water to overflow and flood the floor. Dan stepped in, yelling at Jimmy to leave the bathroom. He then fished out the towel that Jimmy had stuffed into the toilet bowl. Jimmy was hovering at the door as Dan cussed and Judy scurried around, grabbing towels to prevent the water from seeping onto the freshly laid wood floors in the hallway. Judy glanced at her son and noticed a glimmer of satisfaction on his face. This, of course, infuriated her. She shouted at him as he retreated down the hallway.

Would Let, Lift, and Listen be effective with Jimmy? Dan and Judy were looking for specific tools to manage him and I was unsure if they were ready and willing to put in place an entirely different framework. And if they did, would it make the changes they desired?

I agreed to work with them, making no promises that Let, Lift, and Listen would yield positive results. Although I knew it was a foundational approach for all ages and stages, I was unsure if it would work with a nonverbal adult child like Jimmy. Judy and Dan were at their wit's end, so we decided to give it a try.

As always, I started with lift, asking them to list all of Jimmy's strengths. He definitely had some wonderful character traits. Judy and Dan reported that he was outgoing, friendly, curious, and welcoming, and that he thrived on attention. They believed that he understood their verbal communication, even if they weren't entirely sure of the extent of his comprehension. They suspected he grasped more than they gave him credit for.

They also reported that he absolutely relished going on outings with his dad. It didn't matter where they went—a trip to the grocery store, the library, the car wash. Any excursion brought joy to Jimmy.

Listening to Jimmy was a bit more difficult. In the absence of spoken words, they learned to interpret his body language, vocalizations, and tone. It was fairly easy to determine whether he was happy or sad or angry. However, frustration, fear, confusion, curiosity, and other emotions required more attentive observation and listening, which they gradually developed over time.

Upon reflecting on the incident with the clogged toilet, they realized it had occurred on a day when Jimmy was bored. There had been no outings that day, and Judy and Dan had been preoccupied with their own tasks remodeling the house. They also noticed that Jimmy liked to be in control. Being responsible for making his parents run around, cuss, and yell certainly gave Jimmy a feeling of control.

Dan and Judy started putting in more effort to really focus on and understand Jimmy's needs, making sure that they didn't let too much time pass without taking him out and giving him their complete attention. They also practiced maintaining a calm, unruffled demeanor when Jimmy misbehaved.

These changes all lessened his mischievous activities, though his curiosity, playfulness, and desire for attention still got him in trouble sometimes. When he caused a major problem, they discovered that letting the consequences do the teaching worked quite effectively. On the day that Jimmy moved everything from the refrigerator into the bathtub, Judy and Dan were ready. They responded with empathy. "Oh no! This is too bad. Now we have to spend all our time putting everything back instead of going to the store." Jimmy understood.

As time passed, Jimmy's behavior improved, and the overall atmosphere in their home became more peaceful and relaxed. An additional positive outcome was that Judy no longer had that nagging guilt of being a bad mom because of all the yelling she used to do. That guilt had prevented her from arranging for any daytime help. With a little more room for clarity, she realized that enrolling Jimmy in an adult day care center would be beneficial for everyone involved. Jimmy loved the independence. And with Jimmy engaged at the center, Dan and Judy found themselves with more quality time to cherish and enjoy each other's company.

PLEASE HELP ME MOVE THE PORCH FURNITURE

Jillian was incredibly frustrated with her stepson, Michael. At age eighteen, Michael was about as helpful as a butterbean. Jillian had started dreading Michael's visits to their home. She believed that her husband, Brent, should expect more of Michael. She wanted him to follow through with consequences when he thoughtlessly left his dirty dishes in the family room or refused to clean up after himself.

Fortunately, Jillian understood that, as a stepmother, taking on the role of disciplinarian might only worsen her relationship with Michael and create tension in her marriage. She had done her best to act as a benevolent aunt, allowing Brent to take the lead as the parent.

With company coming for the weekend, Jillian had a pressing need to move some porch furniture. However, she knew that asking Michael for help would likely result in refusal, empty promises to do it later, or complete silence. She wanted to motivate him in a positive way, so she thought about a way to lift him. She said, "I need some muscles back here."

Michael looked at her quizzically.

"I really need a guy with some muscles to help me move some furniture. I just can't lift it," Jillian continued.

Michael immediately headed out to the back porch, muttering to himself, "It can't be that heavy."

After moving several pieces for her, he suddenly paused and asked her with surprise, "How did you manage to get me to do that?"

On a roll, Jillian replied, "Because you're strong and you're just that kind of man."

Not only did their relationship improve that day but also the porch furniture got moved and Michael felt a sense of accomplishment and pride in his growing strength and ability to help.

WE DON'T LIKE OUR DAUGHTER'S BOYFRIEND

Chloe, a twenty-three-year-old who had recently started a new job in a city several hours away from home, introduced her new boyfriend, Chase, to her parents. However, her parents were unimpressed by him. They found Chase to be unmotivated in life and somewhat rude, and he did not treat their daughter with respect. They were puzzled as to why she would choose a man like him. Chloe was an intelligent young woman with dreams of a future with a partner who shared her goals and vision.

Her parents knew they could not make the choice for her, and openly expressing their dislike for Chase or suggesting that she could do better might only push her toward him. With no control over her choice of friends, they pondered how they could best influence her.

Chloe's parents understood that people with a strong sense of self-worth tend to expect others to treat them with worthiness as well. Perhaps they needed to lift her a bit more. They also considered the importance of genuinely listening to her. They knew that when she processed things out loud, she often arrived at new realizations.

The next time Chloe came home for a visit alone, they rolled out the red carpet. There were flowers in her room and her favorite snacks in the refrigerator. They planned a special evening at her favorite restaurant. In every possible way, they conveyed their deep love and appreciation for her and that she was valued as a person. They looked for opportunities to notice and acknowledge specific things she was doing well, both presently and in the past.

They also gave her many opportunities to talk. At one point, she mentioned being invited on a ski weekend with her college friends. Her mother commented on how much fun it sounded and how wonderful it was that Chloe had a job that paid her what she was worth, enabling her to afford such a trip. Chloe admitted that she had declined the invitation.

Knowing that bombarding Chloe with questions tended to shut her down, her mother refrained from asking why she wasn't going skiing. Instead, she said, "That's a surprise. You love to ski, and those are your good friends!"

Chloe continued to talk and eventually revealed that her boyfriend didn't want to go because he couldn't afford it and he didn't know any of her friends. Chase also didn't want Chloe to go on the trip.

Mom empathized and kept listening, resisting the urge to say, "Go yourself and leave this guy behind." Wisely she refrained from offering advice or expressing her opinion without being asked.

Chloe then mentioned, "I suppose I could go without him. I just wish Chase wanted to join me. I even offered to pay for his trip."

In response, her mom said, "That's an interesting idea. What do you think would happen if you went without Chase?"

Chloe contemplated the idea. "Well, I know I would have a great time. But Chase would be mad." There was a pause before Chloe continued, "And why should he be? I offered to cover his expenses."

Mom patiently listened as Chloe continued to talk about how unfair Chase's behavior was.

Finally, Chloe expressed, "Mom, I just don't know what to do." Her mother smiled inwardly, realizing that by providing her daughter with the space and an opportunity to talk, Chloe was carefully considering her options and voicing the same things her mom was thinking.

Eventually, Mom said, "Chloe, you have always made good decisions. You have goals, you have ideas, and you have a bright future ahead of you. You will know if Chase cares for you the way you deserve. I know you will figure this out."

On the day Chloe was leaving, her father asked if he could take her out to lunch. Chloe hesitated, wondering if her dad intended to lecture her or give her advice, as he often did when he wanted alone time with her. She reluctantly agreed.

Chloe was pleasantly surprised. Her dad treated her as an adult. He expressed genuine curiosity about her job and found many opportunities to lift and encourage her. He offered no advice. As he hugged her goodbye, he even called her princess, a pet name he had given her many years ago. Chloe drove back to her new hometown feeling loved, honored, and even a little like princess royalty.

Although Chloe did not join her friends on the ski trip, her contemplation about the situation left her feeling angry and sad. She knew she deserved a partner who treated her with greater kindness. Eventually, she decided to end the relationship with Chase.

While there had been no guarantee that a breakup would happen, Chloe's parents knew that they could have the greatest influence on their daughter by lifting and listening. They figured that Chloe had also learned from the consequences of listening to Chase and missing a great trip with her friends.

MAY I GO TO MEXICO?

Lilly called her mother, Katherine, from college to ask if it would be okay if she went to Mexico with a friend for the Christmas holidays. With a stab of pain at the thought of missing her child over the holidays, Katherine listened as best she could as she reeled at the thought of the holidays without her daughter. Still recovering from her recent divorce, Katherine knew the holiday season would be difficult. Now this.

Lilly proceeded to describe the amazing opportunity. She and her friend would be staying with her friend's aunt, who had been living in Mexico for several years. After ensuring the safety of the plan, Katherine took a deep breath and replied very honestly. "Everything inside me wants to say no because I would miss you so much. However, if I were you and had an opportunity like this, I would take it. Yes, you may go."

With a whoop of excitement, Lilly then shared that Dad had offered to cover half the cost of her plane ticket. Katherine started fuming. Was the expectation for her to cover the remaining cost? Her ex-husband had so much more money than Katherine and tended to outshine her with lavish gifts to Lilly. Their differing approaches toward indulging their daughter had been a long-standing source of conflict throughout their marriage. As Katherine remained silent, it occurred to her that she hadn't been able to change him in the past and certainly couldn't change him now.

Although she was tempted to respond with bitterness or defensiveness, Katherine remembered that lifting others, even her ex-husband, was never a bad move. She knew Lilly was well aware of the contrasting lifestyles her parents led and didn't need a reminder of the conflict or differences. Lilly didn't deserve to be burdened with her mother's situation or hurt feelings. None of this was Lilly's responsibility.

Taking a deep breath, Katherine responded, "Wow. Daddy is incredibly generous to you. That's wonderful. How do you plan to cover the other half?"

"I don't know, Mom," Lilly replied. "That's a problem. I really shouldn't exhaust all my savings on this trip."

"Well, Lilly, you are a wise and resourceful young lady. I'm confident you'll figure out what to do. I love you."

The following day, Lilly called again, bursting with excitement. "Guess what, Mom? Daddy offered to pay for the other half of my trip."

"That's fantastic, Lilly. He is beyond generous. I'm so happy for you."

As Katherine hung up the phone, conflicting emotions flooded her. She was sad about missing Lilly at Christmas. She was angry at her ex-husband's ability and willingness to spend so much money on their daughter when she couldn't. Additionally, she experienced frustration, believing it would have been a more valuable growth experience if Lilly had contributed at least a portion of the expenses.

Katherine knew these emotions were better discussed with a trusted adult, not her nineteen-year-old child. Contemplating her mature response, she felt strong and confident in her decision to take the high road for the sake of her precious daughter.

CHAPTER 10

Sibling Dynamics

SEND THAT BABY BACK TO THE HOSPITAL

Haley was such a sweet and happy three-year-old. She was excited about her baby brother, Kalen, and proudly shared the news with everyone she met, proclaiming, "I'm a big sister!" Her parents were overjoyed with the way she hugged and loved her new little brother. They had always hoped for a sibling for Haley, and everything seemed to be falling into place. They had done all the right things, such as reading books about welcoming new siblings, transitioning Haley to her big girl bed, and ensuring she received plenty of one-on-one attention.

They were quite unprepared when her hugs got a little tight and Haley started getting rough with Kalen. One day, to her mother's horror, Haley pinched Kalen's cheek so hard that he burst into tears. Mom swiftly scooped up Kalen to comfort him as she spoke sharply to Haley and sent her to her room. Mom continued comforting and cooing to poor, innocent Kalen. When Kalen fell asleep, Mom tucked him safely in his crib and headed to Haley's room to have a little talk.

Mom was shocked when she discovered that Haley had ripped up one of her books and thrown all her dollies on the floor. At that moment,

Mom was too overwhelmed to listen or lift Haley. She took a deep breath, managed to muster an empathetic *oh no*, and quickly shut the door.

Breathing deeply, she thought about what had just happened. She instinctively understood that Haley was hurting due to the extra attention Kalen was receiving. Reflecting on the incident, Mom realized that when Haley had lost control and pinched Kalen, she had been sent to her room alone while she overheard Mom lavishing attention on Kalen. It must have been incredibly tough for Haley.

Mom slowly allowed compassion to rise and replace the anger she initially felt toward Haley. She took a few more deep breaths, reentered the room, and embraced Haley tightly. She offered a door opener by commenting, "You're really upset."

Haley looked back at her mother, her face expressing a mix of anger, fear, and sadness.

Mom made a conscious effort to listen with all her senses. Finally, Haley spoke. "I hate Kalen. Take that baby back to the hospital."

Mom didn't want Haley to feel like this. Her inclination was to explain why it wasn't nice to say such things and even to tell Haley that she didn't really mean it. However, she remembered the importance of truly listening and acknowledging Haley's feelings. Instead of telling her young daughter how she should feel, Mom listened and responded, "You don't like Kalen and you want to send him back."

Haley looked at her. "Not forever. Just for now."

Mom responded with more compassion and understanding, Finally, Haley threw herself into her mother's arms as sobs shook her little body.

At that inopportune moment, Kalen woke up and began crying. Knowing that he was safe in his crib, Mom forced herself to ignore his cries. In this moment, she was certain that Haley's needs were more pressing than Kalen's.

Hearing Kalen's cries, Haley stopped her own sobbing for a moment and glanced up at her mom.

"He's okay," Mom soothed. "Right now, I'm hugging you."

Eventually Haley calmed down, and Mom asked, "Shall I help you pick up your dollies?"

Haley sniffled as the two of them tidied up the mess she had made. Although Kalen's cries tugged at Mom's heart, she responded to Haley's distress with compassion, allowing him to cry. Mom and Haley tucked the dollies safely back into their toy bed.

"Look how gently you handle your baby dolls," Mom remarked, then asked Haley if she would like to accompany her to check on Kalen.

Haley would always long for the time when she was the only one. Yet as her parents remained aware and accepting of her feelings and made certain that Haley was treated with as much love and concern as Kalen, Haley was better able to manage her emotions.

BROTHERLY LOVE/HATE

Mom and Dad were concerned about Colson, their eight-year-old son, and his behavior toward his six-year-old brother, Max. They had always believed that their sons were simply engaging in typical sibling fights. They also seemed to have fun together. However, recently Colson's angry attacks appeared to be getting worse, despite their pleas for him to stop.

To address the issue, Mom and Dad tried implementing logical consequences, such as separating the boys when they fought or taking away the object of their dispute. They made an effort to listen to both boys, but it usually resulted in each one complaining about and blaming the other. None of their attempts seemed to be effective, and given that Colson was significantly bigger and stronger than Max, the fights appeared unfair. Mom and Dad found themselves getting increasingly angry with Colson.

After some reflection, Mom and Dad realized that they might not be fully understanding the situation. They considered what it must feel like for the oldest child when a younger sibling is introduced into the family. It occurred to them that younger siblings have always shared the parents' attention but not the oldest child. Perhaps Colson might need more one-on-one time with each parent.

They also began to suspect that Max might be deriving some satisfaction from seeing his big brother get in trouble. This reminded Mom and Dad of their own experiences of enjoying getting their older siblings in trouble when they were younger. Was it possible that Max had learned to taunt Colson to get a reaction out of him and that he enjoyed watching his big brother get in trouble? Mom and Dad resolved to pay even closer attention to what was going on.

Mom and Dad also took note of the timing of the conflicts. They decided to become more proactive by using distractions and redirection.

Now when the boys fight, Mom or Dad gently intervenes and sends them both in separate directions, refusing to take sides or entertain blaming. They recognize that when the boys' emotions run high, their ability to think logically diminishes. Once the boys have calmed down, Mom and Dad sometimes speak with them individually, brainstorming ways they can handle situations more effectively. They understand that sibling conflict is normal, and in addition to reducing its frequency, they have learned to help their children grow through the process.

CHARLIE INTERFERES

Thomas, who was fourteen-years-old, and his twelve-year-old brother, Cameron, usually got along, although they did have their moments of disagreement that sometimes turned physical. One day Thomas's friend Charlie was at their house, and the three of them were getting ready to play a video game. Their mother was in another room, but she noticed that the volume and tone of the boys' voices got a bit heated. Initially she ignored it, but when the noise became too much, she peeked her head into the family room and sweetly asked if the boys needed her help solving their problem.

Charlie immediately responded, ready to explain how Cameron had been at fault, but he was quickly cut off by both Cameron and Thomas, who told him to be quiet. They turned to their mom and said, "No thanks, Mom. We can figure this out."

Mom responded, "Great! The noise was starting to bother my ears. I hope you can figure it out. I'm always here to help." She smiled and left the room.

As she walked away, she overheard the boys explaining to Charlie, "If Mom solves our problem, you'll have to go home, and we'll probably be banished outside." They then proceeded to come up with a way to share the game.

Mom had learned that trying to referee or take sides in her children's arguments was futile. She had taught her boys how to negotiate and cooperate, and when they forgot to use these skills, she was quick to make a plan that neither of her boys liked.

TEESHA DESTROYS JAMAL'S FORT

Six-year-old Jamal had spent an hour constructing a special fort when his younger sister, Teesha, entered his room and tore it down. Filled with anger and frustration, Jamal yelled at her and pushed her down, hard.

Mom, arriving just in time to witness the push, swiftly scooped up her crying darling and yelled at Jamal. "How many times do I have to tell you to be nice to your little sister? She's smaller than you. Now clean up this mess." As she walked away with Teesha in her arms, the little darling flashed a smile at Jamal.

Parenting Tip: Sibling Conflict

We seldom know for certain exactly what happened during a sibling fight or argument. There is no way to truly grasp the entire story. Parents who witness only a fraction of the conflict or attempt to gather all the facts and pass judgment often exacerbate the situation. Even if a parent can determine who is to blame, children possess a remarkable ability to provoke each other, hoping to gain parental favoritism. Loving parents address the problem without assuming the role of judge and jury.

When dealing with sibling conflict, the goal is to maintain harmony within the family and to guide your children in developing problem-solving skills. Individually, you might spend time listening to each child, helping them brainstorm how they might handle similar situations in the future.

In the story of Jamal and Teesha, a better response might be this: "It looks like the two of you are having difficulties getting along. Do you need to spend time alone in your rooms?"

Later, after the children have been separated for an appropriate amount of time and considering each of their needs, the mom could go to each of their rooms individually.

After listening to Jamal and acknowledging his frustration with having his fort knocked down, perhaps she will help him brainstorm better ways to handle such situations. Additionally, she might offer him a designated space where he can build a fort without the risk of Teesha destroying it.

In response to Teesha, the mom could tend to her minor injury with care and affection. She could then inquire how Jamal might feel after putting so much effort into building the fort. They could brainstorm ways for Teesha to make amends for destroying her brother's fort.

CONCLUSION

As you have read these stories, you have witnessed how the Let, Lift, and Listen framework can be applied to various situations involving different families and children. Invariably, parents who incorporate this framework into their family dynamics share that they also use it with their spouses, friends, relatives, neighbors, and coworkers. Remarkably, all their relationships are improving.

Why is this framework so effective? When practiced with an attitude of love, it is genuine, honest, and respectful. It is not merely a new technique or a means to manipulate others. It is treating others the way we wish to be treated, regardless of their age or station in life.

Letting logical consequences teach lessons reflects real life. Lifting people with honest and sincere appreciation for who they are encourages them and brings out their best qualities. Listening with the intention to genuinely understand their words and emotions is an act of love and kindness and fosters deeper connections among individuals.

May you discover immense peace and joy in your life as you continue to *Let, Lift, and Listen*.

Cheering you on,
Coach Christine

ACKNOWLEDGMENTS

Thank you to my four children, T.J., Brian, Bobby, and Amy Grace, who have provided me with forty joyful years of valuable practice. To my husband, Bruce, who exemplifies a good husband and stepfather. To the father of my children, Tom, for wholeheartedly loving our children. To my siblings, Bill, Jen, Mike, and Leslie, for teaching me the essence of being a middle child. To Bill and Laura, for all your creative juices. To Leslie, for all the legal and big sister wisdom. To Gloria Degaetano, founder of the Parent Coaching Institute, for her transformative work that is changing the world. To my fellow mastermind PCI coaches, Rhonda, Adrian, Beth, Mary, Amy, Peggy, Dana, and Cindy, who inspire, teach, and encourage me. To Julie, Christi, and Whitney, for editing and refining my work. To Lisa, Priscilla, Amy, and Stephanie, who have been the kind of friends who love, encourage, and co-parent in any and all circumstances. To Al and SEL4SC, for devoting so much time and attention to our community. To Kathy and Shilah, and the rest of the team at Bublish for their invaluable support in transforming my ideas into a book. To all the parents I have coached and taught, I have learned so much from each of you and am deeply honored and humbled by your trust in me. And to those who are doing all they can to be the best parents they can be, I am cheering you on!

ENDNOTES

1   The Parent Coaching Institute (PCI) provides a graduate-level training program, certifying over 700 professional Parent Coaches throughout the world. Parent Coaching Institute. (n.d.-b). PCI. https://www.thepci.org/

2   This is one of many excellent stories inspired by the experts at the Love & Logic Institute. I highly recommend the book "Love & Logic". Cline, F., & Fay, J. (2020a). *Parenting with Love and Logic*. NavPress.

3   Durrant J, Ensom R. Physical punishment of children: lessons from 20 years of research. CMAJ. 2012 Sep 4;184(12):1373-7. doi: 10.1503/cmaj.101314. Epub 2012 Feb 6. PMID: 22311946; PMCID: PMC3447048.

4   Morris AS, Silk JS, Steinberg L, Myers SS, Robinson LR. The Role of the Family Context in the Development of Emotion Regulation. Soc Dev. 2007 May 1;16(2):361-388. doi: 10.1111/j.1467-9507.2007.00389.x. PMID: 19756175; PMCID: PMC2743505.

5   Robson, L. (2015). *Language of Life-Giving Connection: The Emotional Tone of Language that Fosters Flourishing Campus Sustainability Programs* [Doctoral dissertation, Case Western Reserve University]. OhioLINK Electronic Theses and Dissertations Center.

6   Fredrickson BL, Joiner T. Positive emotions trigger upward spirals toward emotional well-being. Psychol Sci. 2002 Mar;13(2):172-5. doi: 10.1111/1467-9280.00431. PMID: 11934003.

7   *Practical Solutions Parent coaching.* (n.d.-b). Practical Solutions Parent Coaching. https://www.practicalsolutionsparentcoaching.com/

8   Williams, S. (n.d.). *Effective listening.* http://www.wright.edu/~scott.williams/LeaderLetter/listening.htm

9   Haney, William V. *Communication and Interpersonal Relations: Text and Cases/William V. Haney.* 4th ed. Homewood, Ill: R. D. Irwin, 1979. Print.

10 Huseman, R. C., Lahiff, J. M., & Penrose, J. M. (1991). *Business Communication: Strategies and Skills.* Chicago : Dryden Press.

11 Haney, William V. *Communication and Interpersonal Relations: Text and Cases/William V. Haney.* 4th ed. Homewood, Ill: R. D. Irwin, 1979. Print.

12 Smith, D. (2001, October 1). Multitasking undermines our efficiency, study suggests. *Monitor on Psychology*, *32*(9). https://www.apa.org/monitor/oct01/multitask

13 Fromm, E. (2013). *The art of loving.* Open Road Media.

14 Fay, J., & Fay, C. (2000). *Love and logic magic for early childhood: Practical Parenting from Birth to Six Years*

15 US Census Bureau. (2022, November 21). *America's Families and Living Arrangements: 2022.* Census.gov. https://www.census.gov/data/tables/2022/demo/families/cps-2022.html

16 Ryan, Richard M., and Edward L. Deci. "Self-determination theory and the facilitation of intrinsic motivation, social development, and well-being." *American psychologist* 55.1 (2000): 68.

17 Cline, F., & Fay, J. (2020a). *Parenting with Love and Logic*. NavPress.

18 Baker, K. B. (2023, March 29). Please Don't Help My Kids. *Milford, MA Patch*. https://patch.com/massachusetts/milford-ma/s/65u0e/moms-plea-please-dont-help-my-kids

19 Arain M, Haque M, Johal L, Mathur P, Nel W, Rais A, Sandhu R, Sharma S. Maturation of the adolescent brain. Neuropsychiatry Dis Treat. 2013;9:449-61. doi: 10.2147/NDT.S39776. Epub 2013 Apr 3. PMID: 23579318; PMCID: PMC3621648.

20 Johnson, S. B., Blum, R., & Giedd, J. N. (2009). Adolescent Maturity and the brain: The promise and pitfalls of neuroscience research in adolescent health policy. *Journal of Adolescent Health*, 45(3), 216–221. https://doi.org/10.1016/j.jadohealth.2009.05.016

21 SAME AS NOTE (20)

RECOMMENDED RESOURCES

Letting the Consequences Do the Teaching

Cline, Foster and Fay, Jim, (2020), *Parenting with Love & Logic: Teaching Children Responsibility*, Navpress

Greene, R. W. (2017). *Raising Human Beings: Creating a Collaborative Partnership with Your Child*. Simon and Schuster.

Mogel, W. (2008). *The Blessing Of A Skinned Knee: Using Jewish Teachings to Raise Self-Reliant Children*. Simon and Schuster.

Lifting With Honest Appreciation

Dyer, W. W. (2010). *What Do You Really Want For Your Children?* Harper Collins.

Tsabary, S. (2010). *The Conscious Parent: Transforming Ourselves, Empowering Our Children*. Namaste Publishing.

<u>Listening With Open Ears, Hearts, and Minds</u>

Brackett, M. (2019). *Permission to Feel: Unlocking the Power of Emotions to Help Our Kids, Ourselves, and Our Society Thrive.* Celadon Books.

Chapman Foundation for Caring Communities. (2023, June 30). *Home - Chapman Foundation for Caring Communities.* https://www.chapmancommunities.org/

Chapman, G., & Campbell, R. (2016). *The 5 Love Languages of Children: The Secret to Loving Children Effectively.* Moody Publishers.

Discover Your Love Language® - The 5 Love Languages®. (n.d.). Northfield Publishing. https://www.5lovelanguages.com/

Faber, A., & Mazlish, E. (2012). *How to Talk So Kids Will Listen & Listen So Kids Will Talk.* Simon and Schuster.

<u>General Parenting</u>

Miller, B., Funari, M., & Armstrong, A. (2021). *Real-Time Parenting: Choose Your Action Steps for the Present Moment.* Real Time Parenting.

<u>Gender Differences</u>

Sax, L., MD PhD. (2007). *Why Gender Matters: What Parents and Teachers Need to Know about the Emerging Science of Sex Differences.* Harmony.

Sax, L. (2016). *Boys Adrift: The Five Factors Driving the Growing Epidemic of Unmotivated Boys and Underachieving Young Men.* Hachette UK.

Sax, L. (2020). *Girls on the Edge: Why So Many Girls Are Anxious, Wired, and Obsessed—And What Parents Can Do.* Hachette UK.

Medications

Kalikow, K. T. (2011). *Kids On Meds: Up-to-Date Information About the Most Commonly Prescribed Psychiatric Medications.* W. W. Norton & Company.

Motivation

Dweck, C. S. (2007). *Mindset: The New Psychology of Success.* Ballantine Books.

Technology

Humanetechnology.com. (n.d.). https://humanetechnology.com/ (Specifically, the "resources for parents/students section)

INDEX TO COMMON ISSUES

Parent Guilt/Parent Fails

Sibling Conflict

Single Parents

Special Needs Children

Sports

ABOUT THE AUTHOR

Christine Donavan lives on the Isle of Palms near Charleston, South Carolina. As a PCI Certified Parent Coach and Certified Collaborative Divorce Parenting Expert, she has guided and empowered parents throughout the world. She works with parents of children from newborn through adulthood and is a frequent speaker and presenter at schools, churches and conferences. She is a former newspaper columnist, director of nonprofits for children, youth pastor, author of family guidebooks in cities throughout the country and has served on the board of directors of several family-focused non-profits. She is recognized locally and nationally as the parent educator who identified the Let, Lift, & Listen framework for parenting. Christine is a mother of four, stepmother of four, and grandmother of seven. She is passionate about helping good parents become great parents.

Made in the USA
Columbia, SC
28 October 2023

25100457R00100